As a wildlife professional, it's a passionate about their sport. fishing, especially flyfishing. H by decades of journaling, makes me regret that I haven't journaled my own outdoor adventures. Through many great stories, the author clearly shows his love for fishing as well as his love for family and friends.

Rod Smith
Oklahoma Department of Wildlife Conservation

Having known Tom for more than 20 years, many of these trips are part of my memories as well. Tom started with keeping data and using that information in hopes of catching more fish. After reading these pages, I think he found that, more than the data, he has appreciated the pursuit of the fish, but most of all, those whom he had the opportunity to share those times with. No matter how you tell the stories, you find those adventures are getting better as the years go by. Great read. It has me thinking about all the time I have spent on the water, and the rich friendships I have found there.

Tom Adams
Guide, Trip Host & Fly-fishing Instructor

Not your usual How to-Where to, fishing book. A tale gleaned from a lifetime of angling and journaling and the stuff in between. Tom shares his journey from a young lad on farm ponds in Oklahoma to the gloried trout streams of the Rockies. Another reminder that it's the JOURNEY that is the prize – Kudos.

Ed Adams
Fly-fisherman and Journaler

Tom Friedemann is the most interesting fisherman I have met in 20 years covering the outdoors. We all have fish stories, but Tom has the data to back up his tales. He has kept the ultimate fisherman's diary.

Ed Godfrey, Outdoor Editor
The Oklahoman newspaper

IF IT WERE EASY,
THEY'D CALL IT CATCHIN'

How Journaling Can Improve Your Fishing and Yourself

TOM FRIEDEMANN

Archway Publishing books may be ordered through booksellers or by contacting:

Archway Publishing
1663 Liberty Drive
Bloomington, IN 47403
www.archwaypublishing.com
844-669-3957

Because of the dynamic nature of the Internet, any web addresses or links contained in this book may have changed since publication and may no longer be valid. The views expressed in this work are solely those of the author and do not necessarily reflect the views of the publisher, and the publisher hereby disclaims any responsibility for them.

Any people depicted in stock imagery provided by Getty Images are models, and such images are being used for illustrative purposes only. Certain stock imagery © Getty Images.

ISBN: 978-1-4808-9421-1 (sc)
ISBN: 978-1-4808-9423-5 (hc)
ISBN: 978-1-4808-9422-8 (e)

Library of Congress Control Number: 2020914950

Print information available on the last page.

Archway Publishing rev. date: 09/22/2020

This book is dedicated to my lovely wife Cindy who is also my fly-fishing buddy and number one cheerleader for writing this book.

To my children Jim and Kari, their spouses Kimm and Jason; and to my six wonderful grandchildren, Nathan, Jordan, Audrey, Noah, Nicholas, and Olivia who have all brought joy beyond measure to my life as a dad and grandpa.

And to my parents, Adolph and Florence Friedemann, who were as close to being perfect parents as God ever made. Mom created a desire in me to become a fisherman at a very early age by teaching me my favorite nursery rhyme:

> Fishy fishy in the brook
> Papa catch 'em by the hook
> Mama fry 'em in the pan
> Tommy eat 'em like a man

CONTENTS

ACKNOWLEDGEMENTS

I would like to express my appreciation to the following who all played a role in one way or another in writing this book:

Cindy Friedemann, my wife who was always willing to drop everything and read every draft of every chapter and provide valuable feedback and editing.

Jim Friedemann, my son and loyal fly-fishing buddy, who is also my best friend and role model. Someday when I grow up, I want to be just like him.

Alan (A.B.) Friedemann, my cousin and the person who had the biggest impact on me in developing my love for fishing. I wish I could tie flies as good as he does.

Bob Verboon, a gifted taxidermist and world class fly-fisher, who never gave up on me converting 100% to fly-fishing. Two of his mounts that he refused take money for, a 39" pike and 22" rainbow, are hanging in my man cave.

Chuck Nithman, another world class fly-fisher, who gifted me my favorite fly rod for nymph and dry fly-fishing, a 3 weight, 10 foot beauty he made using a TFO blank.

Dave Gillogly, whose book *Fishful Thinking* featuring fishing memories made at his cabin in Silver Gate, Montana, served as a catalyst for me becoming an author.

Bob Perry, superintendent of Gordon Cooper Technology Center, Shawnee, OK and author who gave me valuable advice in getting started with my first book.

Ed Godfrey, outdoor writer for *The Oklahoman*, who

encouraged me to use the data from my 56 years of journaling to write this book.

Maria Veres, Adjunct Instructor at the Francis Tuttle Technology Center, Oklahoma City, OK. Her "Joy Of Writing" class provided me with the necessary skills and desire to become a writer.

Bruce Gray, who left this earth much too early, was my mentor throughout my professional career and the best bass fisherman I ever fished with.

Charles Nida, the uncle who took me fishing as a boy to some of the best farm ponds in Logan and Noble Counties in rural Oklahoma.

INTRODUCTION

The year was 1963, and the average price of a new home was $12,650; the Beatles released a future hit, "I Want To Hold Your Hand"; pleatless pants were the fashion rage in men's clothing; and on April 9, a fourteen-year-old farm boy in Oklahoma journaled his first fish—a 1¾ pound largemouth bass caught in a pond on a red-and-white Martin Fly Plug using a Mitchell 304 spinning reel with a solid glass rod. While that last example may have seemed rather insignificant on a national scene that also witnessed the assassination of a president and the escalation of a war in Southeast Asia, it was the beginning of a journey for one young boy that would lead to a life of contentment that would carry him into his seventies and serve as an antidote for the many trials he would encounter in obtaining a college degree, establishing a career, raising a family, and eventually accepting retirement. At first glance, it would appear to be putting a lot of pressure on a simple pastime, but I would submit to you that finding a passion you can wrap yourself up in is an integral part of the American Dream when (1) things don't quite go the way you had dreamed they would or (2) you just want to pursue a little happiness for no reason at all other than because it's just a lot of fun! The importance of having an outside passion really hit home following my divorce after a thirty-one-year marriage to my high school sweetheart. A very dear friend and fly-fishing buddy, Bob Verboon, gave me a gift and signed the card with a handwritten piece of advice that read, "just go fishing and everything will be all right." I followed that advice and found that it is the perfect salve for all the unexpected things that happen to all of us as we pursue a life well lived. I always felt that John Voelker said it better than anybody in his published "Testament of a Fisherman," which reads in part, "I fish because I love to ... not because I regard fishing as being so terribly important but because I suspect that so many of the other concerns of men are equally unimportant—and not nearly so much fun."

The idea of journaling first came to me after reading an article in *Outdoor Life* magazine that was authored by Sam Welch, known back in the sixties as "Mr. Bass" because of his consistent success on Bull Shoals Lake in Arkansas. I thought to myself, "What fun it would be to keep a record of all your fish." I could relive those memories during the cold winter months and use the recorded data to get better the next time I was out on the water—kind of like the way sports teams today use analytics to make decisions on and off the field. So I bought a miniature three-ring binder filled with paper and began my data journey by logging the first decent-size fish I caught in 1963. At the time this book was written, a total of 839 fish have been recorded, along with brief narratives describing the conditions under which they were caught and anything else that I felt would bring joy to my heart. This book is about something that transcends the joy of catching one of God's creatures on an artificial bait. It describes, to the best of my ability, how a hobby can be the one consistent thing in your life that you always look forward to; and even when you can't engage in it directly, you can read about it and relive times that gave you a sense of internal warmth, comfort and joy.

I started out as a fly-fisher, and this was quite by accident. It was 1956, and I was only seven years old, when my maternal grandfather, William Voise, passed away and Grandma gave me his fly reel. I am not sure whatever happened to his fly rod, but I suspect it may have gone to his son, Charles Voise, one of two Uncle Chucks that were in my family. The reel was a

Weber Futurist and was made of that revolutionary new material called Bakelite. What a treasured gift! I had two older male cousins, and to this day I have never figured out why Grandma chose me to give the reel to, but I didn't ask questions and was eternally grateful to her for doing that. After months of saving my weekly allowance, I managed to scrape up enough money to go to the local hardware store and purchase a really cheap solid glass 7½ foot fly rod that had only four guides and a tip-top. The action could best be described as something similar to that of a freshly cut willow branch, but after a few lessons from my other Uncle Chuck (Nida), I managed to get good enough to be able to make roll casts that proved to be effective for bluegill in our Oklahoma farm ponds as well as the stocked trout I would encounter in Missouri's Roaring River State Park during our family's annual vacation taken each August after the plowing was done.

I also learned how to use the fly rod with live bait and a bobber for catfish, and it served me well until one fateful day when my older cousin Alan, whom we all called A. B., came over from his farm just a mile away and introduced me to the dark side with his new fishing rig he had just purchased. For the first time in my life, at age nine, I saw something called a spinning rod and reel, and I was fascinated by this new technology. Wow! He could cast that ¼ ounce casting plug a mile with only the flick of a wrist. I had to get me one of those! Imagine—no more messing around with all that excess line to cast and having to time the forward cast just right to load the rod and shoot out the line. This was modern living at its best, and I immediately began to plan a strategy on how I could get one. About that same time, I got a flyer in the mail addressed to me (which for someone my age was a pretty big deal in those days) showing all the prizes someone could win by selling greeting cards. I studied the flyer, and right there it was—a Keystone Jetstream Spinning Reel, complete with a six-foot solid glass rod and six-pound-test monofilament line. I just needed to sell enough cards to earn the points necessary to qualify for it.

Fortunately, I came from a large extended family (twelve siblings on Dad's side and five on Mom's), so I had a bunch of loving uncles and aunts to sell to. After a summer of selling greeting cards for all occasions and a winter of selling Christmas cards to family and friends, I had achieved my goal. The day it came in the mail, I felt like Ralphie when he got his Red Ryder BB gun for Christmas. Could it get any better than this? The reel was made in Japan back when there was a lot of cheap stuff coming out of that country following WWII, and the rod felt like another willow tree branch, but I could get enough distance on it to catch some fish in local farm ponds. The reel quickly wore out after two years of heavy use and abuse by a boy with limited fishing skills, but nonetheless, it still proudly hangs in a shadow box in my man cave as a reminder of those early days, which soon led to my journaling of all my quality fish. The Weber Futurist from Grandpa also is displayed in that same shadow box as a memorial to my first tools of the trade. At age eleven, through more allowance saving, I upgraded to a Garcia Mitchell 304 with a matching Garcia Conolon tubular fiberglass rod, which never did wear out—my first lesson in getting what you pay for!

It wasn't long after the purchase of the Garcia Mitchell spinning rig that I began reading everything I could get my hands on about bass fishing. I had subscriptions to each of the big three publications in hunting and fishing magazines at the time: *Outdoor Life, Sports Afield*, and *Field & Stream*. I also bought the annual fishing magazines from Garcia and other fishing vendors when they came out every spring. The first book I read on fishing was written by Jason Lucas and was titled *Lucas on Bass Fishing*. He was my hero in much the same manner Tom Brady might be to an aspiring young quarterback who wants to someday play in the NFL. I had other heroes as well, including Sam Welch, Homer Circle, Tom McNally, and Gadabout Gaddis. Gadabout had a fishing show on TV every Saturday and would fly his plane to premier fishing locations all over the country. Man, I couldn't wait for Saturdays to come and see where Gadabout would take us next. No cartoons for this kid! The more I read and watched, the more my passion for fishing grew, which soon led to me journaling my quality fish, ala Sam Welch. As Christopher Camuto, writer for Trout Unlimited, so aptly said, "Every fishing day is worth recording or remembering on the page as a record of a forgiving time-honored way of making sense of things." For me, the world just seemed to make more sense when I was out on the water. And journaling my experiences later seemed to bring me countless hours of pleasure and enjoyment long after the trip, which also made me a better fisherman, and, I hope, a better person.

This book is a little bit about what it was like to grow up on a farm in Oklahoma, a little bit about finding something really fun to do in that environment once the farm work was done, and a whole lot about the role journaling can play in magnifying the satisfaction that comes when one of God's creatures gives you the ultimate compliment of taking your artificial fly or lure because he thought it was prey. Think about it: In the case of trout, for example, you're matching your acquired expertise and skill with fifty-six million years of the evolution of his species just to survive. That's a heck of a head start they have on us. Even the most skilled anglers will tell you it's rarely easy. Heck, if it were easy, they'd call it "catchin'"!

CHAPTER ONE

MY HEROES HAVE ALWAYS BEEN FISHERMEN

With apologies to Willie Nelson's hit country song, my heroes have always seemed to be fishermen, and the things I learned from them are still reflected today in the way I approach both fishing and life in general. I feel compelled to begin my list of heroes with Jesus, who, among other notable talents, may have been the first fishing guide ever written about. On Lake Gennesaret, he told two frustrated professional fisherman, Simon and Andrew, where to cast their nets for some good fish, and they wound up catching so many that their boat began to sink! (Luke 5:1–11). Fifteen hundred years later, there was the leader of the Protestant Reformation, Martin Luther, who liked to fish. Luther and his colleague Philip Melanchthon were engaged in a deep theological conversation when Melanchthon turned to Martin Luther and announced, "Today you and I shall discuss the governance of the universe." Luther looked at Melanchthon and said, "No. Today you and I shall go fishing and leave the governance of the universe to God." In my heart, I know he said that to clear his mind so he could begin the most significant religious and political movement in history of the civilized world.

Other heroes include yet another notable fishing guide, Sam Welch, who first acquainted me to logging bass for more

productive fishing trips. But I probably would not have started
the systematic logging of fish had it not been for another hero,
Cousin A. B., who had started his own journal a few years
earlier. I wanted to be like my older cousin in every respect, so
I, too, began as soon as I had acquired enough fishing skills to
catch fish on a consistent basis. Both of my Uncle Chucks (Nida
and Voise) were heroes, because they were the first adults who
took a special interest in me acquiring the skills necessary to
become successful on the water. Gadabout Gaddis was a true
television celebrity, and I watched his every move every Saturday
on the family TV set, much like an aspiring young point guard
would watch Russell Westbrook today. Jimmy Houston, a fellow
Oklahoman, who had made the big time on the national B.A.S.S.
circuit and on television, came to be an influencer on my life
and on my acquisition of fishing skills. His book *Catch of the
Day* does a wonderful job of combining fishing tips with lessons
for spiritual growth. Jason Lucas, a longtime sports editor for
Sports Afield magazine and author of the first book I ever read on
fishing, *Lucas on Bass Fishing*, was among my earlier influencers.
The first fishing tip I ever read about and used as a boy and still
works like a charm to this day, on poppers, is found on page 66.
Mr. Lucas instructs the reader to let the popper lie for a few
seconds before making the first twitch with the rod tip and then
pause a little bit longer before twitching it again. If by the third
time there isn't a strike, the angler should go to another spot.
It's hard to discipline yourself to refrain from making the cast
and immediately begin making those little explosions with your
popper, but the times I've been able to do what Lucas suggests,
it has seemed to work more often than not. Lucas was a master
at all types of fishing, and when I went back to using the fly rod
exclusively, I reread the chapters he devoted to fly-fishing, and
his advice was just as good in the '90s as it was in the '40s. And
I admired President Herbert Hoover so much for his homespun

fishing philosophy and his passion for the sport. According to renowned fishing guide Calvin Albury, President Hoover was the best bonefish angler he had ever seen. One of my favorite fishing quotes is credited to Hoover: "All men are equal before fish." This has helped me get through some ego issues on those days when nothing seemed to work. Hoover was an active fisherman well into his eighties, which should be all the evidence one needs for measuring his passion for the sport.

Another quote from a president that I can really relate to comes from Jimmy Carter, who said his conversion to fly-fishing "was one of the most gratifying developments of [his] life." To further the case for putting President Carter on the hero list is the fact that First Lady Rosalynn Carter was also an avid fly angler; the couple were often seen together on the water during family vacations and on local lakes and ponds in Georgia. I can certainly relate to this, as I'm convinced that one of the reasons I married my lovely wife Cindy was because she, too, is a passionate fly angler. Our early acquaintance came about when she and two of her friends wanted to learn how to fly fish and thus combined their resources to make the winning bid at a United Way auction where I was offering flycasting lessons as part of a fundraising effort at work. She's been in love with the sport—and, fortunately, with me—ever since. Want proof? She cried tears of joy when I gave her a new R. L. Winston fly rod for Christmas—something she had wanted for years. How many wives do you know who would do that? Like the president and Rosalynn, Cindy and I have spent many hours on the water together, pursuing everything from native cutthroats near our cabin in Red River, New Mexico, to sight casting for carp on Taylor Lake near Rush Springs, Oklahoma. She obviously was my catch of the day!

My catch of the day, Cindy and me on an
anniversary trip to Oklahoma's Blue River

Another hero would have to be Bruce Gray, a very dear friend who was also a professional mentor to me in the field of career technical education. I would never have risen professionally to become the superintendent and CEO of one of top career-tech school systems in the country without his guidance and support, and I will ever be indebted to him for always having faith in me. Bruce was one of those guys who seemed to be on the winning team no matter what he set his hand to, including being a star basketball player at both the high school and college levels, being a hall of fame educator, and being one of Oklahoma's most successful bass tournament fishermen and guides on Lake Eufaula. Bruce and I spent many hours fishing for bass all over Oklahoma, and we made annual trips to Canada. He and his brother-in-law, Jim Smith, another gifted fisherman, who was the fire chief in Stillwater, Oklahoma, would have an influence on me beyond measure both as a fisherman and as a human being. It was Jim who came up with a quote that was a catalyst for me developing my personal wall of fame, where I display all the various fish I've been able to catch on a fly rod. The quote just came out one day when Jim, Bruce, and I were all in the same bass boat in Canada. Bruce was a bass purist in every sense of the word, and when we went to Canada, they were his only target. But unfortunately for Bruce, pike and walleye often hit on the same lures that smallmouths were attracted to. Walleyes were somewhat acceptable because they were such a good table fish, but pike—now, that's a different story for a number of reasons. First, they are very difficult to filet because of their dreaded Y bone. Second, they are slimy as all get out and a mess to deal with once you land one. Third, they often will cut your monofilament line with their razor-sharp teeth, causing you to lose a perfectly good bass bait. And lastly, they are usually long, hard fighters that take up a lot of valuable time that could be used in pursuing prized smallmouths. On this day, Bruce had hooked up with a really big, nasty pike that he always referred to as "gaspergoos," and after about ten minutes of a continuous string of obscenities from Bruce, Jim had heard enough and came up with this classic line that I often quote: "Ah hell, Bruce, you just came up here to get your pole bent." Bruce just laughed, because there was a lot of wisdom and truth to that comment. And Jim was exactly right. That's why all of us were there in the first place—to enjoy the challenge of achieving the hook-up and the fight of the fish, regardless of whether it was a walleye, smallmouth, pike or, muskie. We were all there to get our poles bent as many times as possible in some of the most beautiful surroundings on the continent. At the end of the day, what difference did it make what kind of Latin description we Earthlings used to describe the fish's family? Words of wisdom indeed!

As far as pure fly anglers go, nobody can top another Oklahoma native, Dave Whitlock. Dave, of course, is a noted author and fly tier, as well as an accomplished artist. I have read everything I can get my hands on that he has written, and one of my most prized possessions in my man cave in Jones, Oklahoma, is an autographed print from him that he signed at a local Trout

Unlimited meeting several years ago in Oklahoma City. It's a reprint of a painting that he did featuring a smallmouth bass trailing a carp feeding on crawfish, and he signed it, "Yours Tom, In Carpin & Smallmouthin." This was after a great conversation we had about fly-roddin' for carp. In my opinion, there isn't anybody out there more knowledgeable about fly-fishing than Dave Whitlock, and hearing him give a presentation is always such a joy and privilege.

CHAPTER TWO
UNCLE CHUCK

Every little boy needs an Uncle Chuck, and as I mentioned in the introduction, I had two of them: Uncle Charles Voise, my mother's brother; and Uncle Charles Nida, who married one of my mother's sisters, Emma. Both Uncle Chucks loved the outdoors and loved to fish and hunt. And while both of them would take me with them to fish from time to time, it was Uncle Chuck Nida who really had an impact on me and helped to nurture my love of fishing.

Uncle Chuck and Aunt Emma lived in Orlando, Oklahoma, a very small town of fewer than three hundred people and about a forty-minute drive from my parents' farm. Uncle Chuck was the town's postmaster and also ran one of the rural mail delivery routes, so he knew every decent farm pond in the area and was known and loved by everybody in the community. He was a WWII Purple Heart veteran and one of the nicest, most humble men you could ever meet. He was truly a wonderful example of America's greatest generation. Uncle Chuck and Aunt Emma never had children of their own, so they were quick to adopt the children of their siblings as their own kids and spoiled all the cousins rotten.

Getting to go to their house for a week in the summer was like getting to go to Disney World, church camp, and the zoo, all wrapped into one! This is what a typical day at their place would look like: In the morning, after a big breakfast, Uncle Chuck would go to work at the post office, and then Aunt Emma would have me do minor chores around the house or run errands for her; she would always pay me exorbitant wages for doing so, and I loved every minute of it. One of my favorite things she would do is ask me to take the short walk to the town's only store, Chadwicks, and buy her some groceries. She would always send me with plenty of money and tell me to keep the change, which was always substantial. And instead of sending me with a single big list of items for a one-time purchase, she would break her needs up into multiple trips so I could go multiple times each day. I would then spend most of the extra change on fishing lures. As a result of her generous strategy, I always left Orlando with an updated inventory of Hula Poppers, River Runts and Lucky 13s. Then Uncle Chuck would come home after lunch and pick me up to ride along with him on his mail route. Man, was that ever fun! He'd point out the various farm ponds that we were going to fish later that day, and my excitement would grow to a fever pitch in anticipation of all the good fishing that was to come.

Each evening after supper, we'd fish, and Uncle Chuck would teach me everything I needed to know about casting, catching and landing fish. Sometimes, if the weather was bad and we didn't get to fish, he'd take me to his basement—today we'd call it his man cave—and show me all his flies and lures. Looking at his vast collection was almost as fun as fishing itself. He'd carefully show me each one, point out its unique features, and explain what it was used for. He would often say to me, "Tommy, do you like that one? Keep it; it's yours!" It was his way of culling his inventory and at the same time making a nephew very happy.

I remember one time when we wet-waded a pond to get beyond the surface vegetation and Aunt Emma took a picture of me with my wet clothes, holding a stringer of fish. Later, when my parents saw the picture, they were really upset because I hadn't learned how to swim yet; I'm sure they both probably had some words with Uncle Chuck later. But that incident proved to be the catalyst for me getting to take swimming lessons later that same summer at Crystal Plunge, the local swimming pool. If you're going to be in the water, you'd better learn how to swim!

Now, my mom and dad were wonderful people, and my younger sister, Susan, and I grew up in the perfect family setting, nurtured by unconditional love that was combined with the necessary discipline it takes to get one ready for life as an adult. When you grow up on a farm, you have a stay-at-home mother as well as a stay-at-home father, so the family bond is about as strong as it can possibly get. When I did something bad at home, Mom never had to say, "Wait until your father gets home." Rather, she would tell me to march across a plowed field and tell my father what I had done. Punishment was always swift and just, and I know my sister and I are better people for it.

Mom and Dad, however, never had any hobbies that weren't directly tied to either generating family income or producing food. They both loved to garden (food production). Dad loved restoring junked Ford 8N tractors and then selling them for a nice profit (family income). And mom loved to sew and would make dresses, uniforms, and wedding gowns, and do men's alterations (family income). I don't think they ever really understood hobbies that didn't produce food or income. A closer look at their backgrounds might shed some light here. They were both first generation German Lutherans born in this country, and their lives were all about working and making the farm productive so Susan and I could have the things they never had. They loved me and my sister beyond measure and instilled in us the values that we still live by today, but to them fishing and hunting were only means of putting food on the table. They never really understood the concept of catch-and-release fishing. So it was great to have an uncle and aunt who treated their nieces and nephews like their grandchildren and had a more modern attitude about the important role hobbies played, and all of us cousins were so fortunate to have them in our lives during our formative years. If there were more Uncle Chucks and Aunt Emmas around, this world would be a better place.

CHAPTER THREE

A RETURN TO MY FLY-FISHING ROOTS

I mentioned in my introduction that I started out as a fly-fisher when I inherited my Grandpa's Weber Futurist fly reel and quickly matched it up with a solid glass unbranded 7½ foot fly rod, but was drawn away, as boys can be, to the flashy long distances my cousin achieved on his spinning reel and soon converted to an easier way to fish. I stayed a spin fisherman and added to my angling arsenal by learning to use a free-spool baitcasting rig, which came in especially handy when fishing in heavy brush with plastic worms with heavier lines. I then took conventional fishing a step further when I purchased a bass boat and began fishing the nearby lakes, and even dabbled a little bit in the world of tournament fishing with some success. But it was competitive tournament fishing that prompted me to question the real reason I chose to fish in the first place. It seemed far too often that I encountered so-called bassmasters who were narcissistic braggers who loved to belittle others' equipment or fishing styles if they differed much from theirs, and they were also tight-lipped as to which lures were successful for them, as well as the productive locations they had found. This was very foreign to me, as most of my fishing to date had been done with very close friends and family members who were freely open with such valuable information. It seemed so strange that these guys were all about themselves and showing the world how great their fishing skills were by proving to everyone that they could catch the largest and most fish.

Now, don't get me wrong; the vast majority of bass fishermen that I met in bass clubs and in tournaments were really fine people. But there were just enough of the undesirables to make fishing not nearly as much fun as it should have been. These types would have done well to contemplate a little bit on the thoughts of Henry David Thoreau, who once said, "Many men go fishing all of their lives without knowing that it is not fish they are after." I think they used fishing as a way to validate their sense of worth to both themselves and their buddies, and catching the biggest and most bass was more important to them than it should have been. To me, most of the fishing pleasure came from just trying to figure it out, seeing whether I could come up with a successful formula for success, and then sharing that knowledge with others. The joy of watching others have success with my methods was part of the fun of fishing. Of course, this especially holds true with one's children and grandchildren.

So I went on fishing in my bass boat with my bubba gear, recording in my fishing log any bass I caught that were 1½ pounds and over for a number of years, all the time feeling as if I was maybe missing something from the total fishing experience. Then I saw "the movie." And many of you reading this book right now know exactly what movie I'm talking about—*A River Runs Through It*, which is based on a story written by Norman Maclean and stars Tom Skerritt, Brad Pitt, et.al., and was directed by Robert Redford. It came out in 1992, and it literally changed my life from a fishing perspective. As I was sitting in the movie theater watching it, I began to have all those familiar warm and fuzzy feelings of sublime contentment going back to those early carefree days of fly-fishing next to Uncle Chuck in Roaring River State Park in the pursuit of rainbow trout, or at the family farm pond with my cousin A. B., catching bluegill on a rigged plastic worm or a popper. This is what fishing was supposed to be like, and actually was like at one time in my life, with no bragging about numbers of fish caught, no worries about having the biggest and most powerful boat so I could get to the honey hole before my competition did, no pressure from losing a qualifying bass that might be the difference between finishing first or being out of the money, no worries about making it back to the weigh-in on time or feeling embarrassed because maybe I didn't even scratch that day. It was just a feeling of that nine-year-old innocence that unknowingly had been missing for the past twenty years since I first purchased the bass boat. What I had thought was an evolution of going to more and more sophisticated pieces of equipment and technology was, in fact, taking me away from the real reasons of why I loved to fish so much. In fact, journaling was probably the only part of my fishing endeavors that remained a constant and seemed to be bringing me joy. When I journaled, the feelings of anxieties previously listed seemed to disappear as I concentrated on only the positive things about each productive fishing trip.

The very next day, I located my old original fly rod and reel, went to the pond a short walk from my house, and realized how outdated the old fly rig was and how poor my skills were at trying to cast a simple popper. So I got my Cabela's catalog and ordered a starter fly rod outfit for just under $100. When it arrived, I immediately went back out to the pond and had some success but realized that the flycasting skills that may have adequately served an eight-year-old boy simply would not do if I was going to become a serious fly angler. This was before the days of the internet and YouTube, so I went to the local public library and checked out every book I could find on fly-fishing, as well as Mel

Krieger's instructional VHS video, *The Essence of Flycasting*. Mel does an excellent job of giving the viewer flycasting basics, and I would recommend any of his works for the beginner. Many hours of practice in the backyard had me picking up enough skills so that I could cast well enough to make a reasonable presentation. My first recorded bass on a fly rod finally came on May 8, 1994, using a 2¼" Creme Angle Worm, and it was the beginning of a personal renaissance that had me going cold turkey from conventional gear. I packed up my spinning and baitcasting rigs for permanent storage in our attic, and I have never looked back. For a while I tried fly-fishing from my bass boat with some success, but the call of farm ponds, small lakes, creeks, and rivers always seemed better suited to my new interest in fishing. I sold my bass boat a few years later. Soon afterward, I purchased a hard body Hobie Cat kick boat, which proved to be ideal for local fisheries. Fly-fishing from my Hobie was even more comfortable than the front pedestal seat of my old bass boat, and it was twice as relaxing.

Man, was this next phase of my fishing journey ever going to be fun! It also seemed to put new life into my journaling, and I soon expanded my fish logs to include fish of all species, not just bass. My new goal was to catch as many different species of fish as possible before I passed on to those pristine waters in the sky, and to have a framed picture of each one represented on a special designated wall in my man cave—a wall of fame, if you will. To date, that list of different species numbers forty and contains a diverse group of both cold-water and warm-water fish, all caught on a fly rod using artificial baits, and includes everything from a Rio Grande chub to a flathead catfish, as well as several saltwater species. This was just a new personal wrinkle to the sport! I also recently added a new "Most Grafting Fish" journal, which I will discuss in detail in a later chapter. All this because of one movie. I wonder if Norman Maclean had any idea what impact his writings would have on the sport for so many of us? I wish someone would pen a sequel. If we can have seven *Rocky* movies, it certainly seems we could have at least one more *A River Runs Through It.*

CHAPTER FOUR
THE CASE FOR JOURNALING

It's twenty degrees outside. As I look out my window, I can see our trees bending southward, being forced to yield to a raw thirty-mile-an-hour north wind. It's raining sideways, for crying out loud! And I'm thinking to myself, How can I make the most of an absolutely miserable day? To further frustrate things, I'm looking at the lake outside my window and daydreaming of all the wonderful aquatic creatures that are just yards away from me, submerged in their winter underwater dwellings and waiting for me to once again challenge them for sport with my fly rod. I think of the words of Izaak Walton, who said, "Rivers and the inhabitants of the watery elements are made for wise men to contemplate and for fools to pass by without consideration."

But what do I do today? I've pretty much completed my winter fly-tying to the point that I am satisfied with my inventory for the coming spring. And watching TV has gotten to be ridiculous with all the reality shows, 24/7 politics, and shopping channels. You can only watch *The Andy Griffith Show* reruns so many times! I've never been into watching movies or been much of a book reader, so how can I entertain myself on this absolutely dismal day? Ahh, there are my fish journals to look at! Fifty-six years of wonderful data-generating experiences that warm my heart and bring back memories of days past and pleasant thoughts of days yet to come. So, just for fun, I may take out my first volume, dated 1963 and begin to reflect back on what it was like being fourteen years old and what may have been going on in my mind as I tried to understand why fish behaved as they did and what I did correctly when I was successful. Or I may take out the volume that represents the time when I began fly-fishing for bass again to relive those early years of the conversion. By this time, you may already have diagnosed my problem as having a severe case of fishing fever. I think the authors of *Wit & Wisdom of Fishing* described my incurable condition best when they wrote,

> Recreational anglers fall into one of two groups;
> Casual and dedicated.
> The first group treat fishing as a way to
> unwind from the daily grind,
> get some fresh air and maybe catch a fish now and then.
> The latter group takes it more seriously, and some –
> quite a few—become involved to the point of obsession.
> When not fishing, they read about it, talk
> about it, watch videos, attend courses,
> And join clubs to congregate with other fishing fanatics

With all due respect to the authors of that wonderful piece of charming insight as to why fishermen behave the way they do, I would add one more descriptor to the final sentence: "and study their journals."

This may be the least read chapter of the book because of all the personal fishing data that it contains, but I thought it was important for you to have a reference base to judge what you may and may not want to include in your own fish logs by looking at some of mine. So I've included some randomly selected excerpts from each of my seven volumes of fish entries to give you an idea of the types of data I've been recording throughout the years. This not only enhanced my opportunities for success on my next fishing trip but also provided a memory recap of a time that was filled with joy and contentment. Of course, the data you decide to record is entirely up to you and is dependent upon what your goals may be for keeping records of your fish, but I thought it might be helpful to see the type of data I've been collecting for over fifty years. Enjoy!

FROM THE FIRST BASS VOLUME, LABELED "1963–1972 (FISH 1 THROUGH 108)"

Captain's log (Oops! This isn't *Star Trek*) ... Fisherman's log— April 9, 1963. Fish 1, a largemouth bass caught at 5:30 p.m. using a red-and-white Martin Fly Plug in Linsenmeyer's West Pond located southeast of Stillwater, Oklahoma, in Payne County. It was fair weather. The water was crystal clear, and I was standing on the dam, casting into a strong north wind. The fish weighed 1¾ pounds, and I caught her on my new Mitchell 304 spinning reel using six-pound-test line. Now remember, this was shortly after my conversion from fly-fishing to spin fishing, so the Martin Fly Plug was a holdover from my fly-fishing collection but was one of the few patterns I could cast reasonably well with my spinning rig. More lures and plugs were soon to follow as I saved up my meager allowance.

Let's move on to 1965, where on August 20 I caught my first really nice bass, fish 31, a 4¾ pounder, also in Linsenmeyer's West Pond. This fish was also caught while I was standing on the dam and casting in all directions. I mentioned that the barometer was falling at the time and there was no wind. The weather was cool and damp, just after a rain, and it was 7:00 p.m. when the fish hit. I caught her on a DeLong nine-inch purple plastic worm with a size 3/0 weedless hook inserted in the head. I was using a Zebco 707 Spinning reel spooled up with twelve-pound-test line, and the water in Linsenmeyer's farm pond was still crystal clear. Man, I used to love fishing that pond. I could look into the water and see the bottom.

The next entry, fish 61, I'd like to highlight was recorded on June 18, 1968. This was the first year I began recording stomach contents in an effort to help me better understand the feeding habits of the fish I caught. Back before my catch-and-release days, I usually cleaned and ate everything I caught, mainly because I liked to eat fish and it was free food, and secondly because stomach contents provided me valuable information. Gutting the fish and opening its stomach was just like Christmas morning to me, and I couldn't wait to see what was inside every catch. I selected this particular entry because the fish, while barely qualifying at 1⅝ pounds, it was one of the fattest post-spawn bass I had ever seen, and the reason was because of what she had just eaten. In her stomach was a fresh five-inch bass and a baby snapping turtle about the size of a silver dollar. And she still went after my green-and-white Arbogast TruShad. What an appetite! There was a moderate east wind that day, and the weather was cool and overcast, just after a rain. It was caught in my uncle Bert Friedemann's farm pond at 10:00 a.m. The water was mud-stained, and she was caught on my brand-new Mepps Super Meca spinning reel with twelve-pound-test line.

One of the last entries in that volume, fish 92, is from April 29, 1972, when I recorded a bass that weighed six pounds with a length of twenty-two inches and a sixteen-inch girth. I was really proud of this one, as it was my largest bass yet. I caught her at 9:15 a.m. using a seven-inch purple Fliptail plastic worm. The weather was cool and cloudy, just before a rainstorm hit, and the water was crystal clear. The wind was out of the southeast. She was caught in Stover's Pond just outside Cherokee, Oklahoma, in Alfalfa County, using my Mitchell reel with twelve-pound-test line. I had her mounted, so no stomach contents were recorded.

FROM THE SECOND BASS VOLUME, LABELED "1973–1980 (FISH 109 THROUGH 214)"

The first entry I'd like to highlight in volume II took place on October 13, 1976. Fish 175 was a four pound bass measuring 20" in length with a 12½" girth. She was caught on a brown-and-orange Lil' Tubby with a black tail. I was standing on the dam of the upper Berry Pond, located near our farm. All of a sudden, a wake came from out of nowhere with a bass emerging to nail the lure right at my feet. This is why I love bass fishing—because I never know what to expect. The weather was cool but sunny with no wind. She had a bullfrog in her stomach. The water clarity was listed as semiclear, and she was caught using my Quick 330 spinning reel.

The next entry I selected from this volume, fish 202, was a 3½ pound bass (19" length, 12" girth) caught in Lake Ellsworth, near Lawton, Oklahoma, on June 27, 1979. By this time, I had my bass boat and was doing a lot of lake fishing. I was fishing off Apache Creek in rough water that was unprotected from a moderate south wind. The fish hit a black-and-white buzzbait. The weather was hot and sunny, and I was using my Penn 940 baitcasting reel with seventeen-pound-test line. The bass had two six-inch shad in her stomach.

FROM THE THIRD BASS VOLUME, LABELED "1981–1990 (FISH 215 THROUGH 329)"

An entry from this volume I selected, fish 220, was a 5½ pound bass (21.5" in length and 14.75" in girth) that was caught in Quanah Parker Lake in the Wichita Mountain Wildlife Refuge from my tube floater using a seven-inch purple Fliptail plastic worm at 8:15 p.m. on April 27, 1981. My records say that I was fishing throughout submerged coontail vegetation and among scattered lily pads in about five to six feet of water west of the peninsula in the north end. There was a strong wind out of the southeast at twenty miles per hour, and the water was crystal clear. I described the fish as having a bloody tail, being full of eggs, and having unidentified fish bones in her stomach.

Another entry from this volume lists one of the bass that was responsible for my second-place finish as a guest participant in the Stillwater Bassmasters Club Tournament. Fish 304 was the largest fish caught in the tournament and weighed 4¾ pounds. She was part of a five-fish total weighing twelve pounds and two ounces, and was caught in Sooner Lake, near Ponca City, at 2:35 p.m. on April 21, 1990, on a deep diving Small Fry Shad. I was fishing the riprap in about eight to ten feet of water near the OG&E power plant. The water was clear, and I was using a Shimano Mag SG10 baitcasting reel with ten-pound-test line. Since the fish was released immediately after the weigh-in, no stomach contents could be recorded.

FROM THE FOURTH BASS VOLUME, LABELED "1991–1994 (FISH 330 THROUGH 452)"

Fish 334 was a five pounder caught in Sells Lake near Pauls Valley, Oklahoma. She was caught in the heat of the day (1:00 p.m.) in the middle of summer on July 14, 1991. This was during a period when I carefully observed the solunar tables and would fish those major times regardless of how hot or cold it might be, and this entry is an example of that. I recorded that the major solunar period ended that day at 2:30 p.m. and that I was fishing deep underwater structure from a boat using a 6½" chartreuse-and-white Scissortail plastic worm with a size 4/0 hook rigged Carolina style, using a jerky retrieve. The wind was light and out of the north, and the water was clear. We had a heavy rain the night before. No stomach contents were recorded because this was about the same time I began to release nearly all my fish.

Fish 413 is the first bass recorded in my bass logs that I caught using a fly rod, which would be my exclusive way to catch this marvelous species from now on. This fish weighed 1½ pounds and was caught at 7:00 p.m. on May 8, 1994, in our family farm pond in Payne County. She hit an Orange 2¼" Creme Angle Worm rigged on a two-hook harness with beads and a propeller. This was a rather modest start, but it was the beginning of an adventure that I would never regret. My records show that I was wading the flats of the north end of the pond and that I had lost several other bass on the same pattern. I guess I was still learning how to set the hook on a fly rod. It was sunny but a nice seventy-degree temperature with a light west wind, and the water was clear. The fish was caught on my brand-new starter rig, a Cabela's 789 reel matched to a nine-foot Cabela's 8-weight rod with WF8F line and a four-pound tippet that had just come in the mail a few weeks earlier. I was as proud of this fish as any I had caught in recent years, as it represented a personal breakthrough for me and a foretaste of what it would feel like to catch more and bigger bass in the years to come.

The final entry I selected from this volume, fish 445, was my first big bass on a fly rod—a four pounder caught on September 3, 1994 at 11:15 a.m. in Uncle Bert's pond, just a mile away from our farm. She was caught on an olive #2 Hank Roberts Hair Worm. According to my entry, the weather was a cool and overcast seventy-degree day, the third straight day without sunshine. The wind was moderate and out of the southeast, the water semiclear and dangerously low. I also recorded that Doug Hannon's best fishing moon times were between 10:15 a.m. and 12:15 p.m. Once again, I was using my Cabela's starter fly rig, but this time I increased the tippet size to ten-pound test.

FROM THE FIFTH BASS VOLUME, LABELED "1995–2006 (FISH 453 THROUGH 571)"

Fish 449, was a rare wintertime bass, a 3½ pound largemouth caught February 2, 1997, on a pattern I designed and tied myself, a white #1/0 Pistol Pete–looking pattern with a chartreuse soft plastic curl tail. The fish was caught at 2:45 p.m. as I was wading along the flats of the east shoreline and casting toward sunken timber near the dam of our family farm pond. I mentioned in the log that the fish totally engulfed the fly and was hooked deep in her mouth. The weather was mostly sunny and sixty-two degrees with a ten to twenty-mile-per-hour northeast wind. The water was mud-stained but still semiclear. By this time, I had begun to upgrade my fly rod arsenal somewhat, and I caught this fish using a Martin M6 fly reel on my original starter Cabela's 8/9-weight rod using a fourteen-pound-test tippet.

This next entry is for a smallmouth bass caught in Lake Obabikon in Ontario. My records show fish 550 as being caught on a big #3/0 white bass popper that I found on eBay that was very crudely made. I was casting from the boat toward crevices in slick, submerged rock formations when this smallie shot out from the deep like a guided missile launched from a submarine and savagely attacked the popper. It was a beautiful, sunny eighty-degree day. The water temperature measured sixty-seven degrees. I described the water as tea-stained but clear. The date and time are listed in the log as June 5, 2003, at 1:25 p.m. The rig I was using was my Martin M6 fly reel with, once again, the starter Cabela's 8/9-weight rod with a ten-pound tippet.

FROM THE SIXTH BASS VOLUME, LABELED "2007–2019 (FISH 572 THROUGH 688)"

Another smallmouth bass, fish 603, is the next entry from this volume. This fish was a 1½ pound smallmouth that was caught while fishing for trout in Oklahoma's Blue River in the catch-and-release trophy section. The date was February 29, 2012, and the time was 1:20 p.m. The log indicates that I caught five rainbow trout that day, including two that measured sixteen inches. I caught the bass on a tan $\frac{1}{64}$ ounce woolly bugger type pattern with a gold jig head, which I designed and tied. The difference between my bugger and the directions on YouTube is that mine is tied on a jig hook using wool for the body instead of chenille and a marabou tail that is untrimmed and longer than the fly itself for a better swimming action. I usually tie them in a ginger color and affectionately call them "Ginger Buggers." The weather was described as a sunny and warm seventy-degree day with perfect water flow. The fish was caught on a Ross Cimarron C1 reel spooled with Teeny T-200 sinking-head line with a 4X leader matched with a telescoping DAM 7/8 weight fly rod that I had stored in my backpack since it was a thirty-minute hike to get to the water from the trailhead. I was standing on the first falls downriver from the trailhead entrance and casting straight out to take advantage of the sinking head getting down deep into the huge pool.

Fish #638 was caught in Jim Strate's farm pond just off Highway 74 near Covington, Oklahoma, on April 12, 2017, at 2:20 p.m. It was a largemouth bass and weighed 2¾ pounds, measuring seventeen inches. According to the log, I was fishing from my Hobie Cat kick boat and slowly skipping a #3/0 Orvis Dry Rind Frog on top of green moss piles floating throughout the pond. I would try to put the frog on top of the pile and then just nudge it off, and the bass would rip into it the instant it hit a clearing. I described the water as mud-stained but semiclear, still feeling the effects of seven inches of rain the week before. The weather was mostly cloudy and seventy-eight degrees with a ten-mile-per-hour south wind.

***

Now let's get to another fish log that I began keeping the year I converted to fly-fishing. It's for non-bass species. Since the bass journals had a forty-year head start, I only have two volumes to date but here are some excerpts from the first volume.

***

FROM THE FIRST NON-BASS VOLUME, LABELED "1994–2012 (FISH 1 THROUGH 94)"

Fisherman's log, May 10, 1994. Fish 1, a bluegill, was caught during late evening (no specific time recorded) on a black-and-gray #8 Woolly Bugger that I tied myself. The fish measured eleven inches and was caught while I was wading the flats along the west shoreline of our family farm pond. It was a beautiful day but was still hot even close to sundown. The water is listed as clear, and she was caught on my starter Cabela's rig using a four-pound tippet.

Fish 23 was a red drum (redfish) caught on April 12, 2000, at 2:05 p.m. using a #1 orange-and-chartreuse Clouser Deep Minnow that I tied. She measured 21½" and weighed four pounds. According to my journal, I was wading in the flats off Mustang Island in Port Aransas, Texas, near the first bridge off Highway 361, when I noticed what looked like fish activity near the surface. I blindly began making casts toward that direction, and the fish hit. The water was cloudy, and the wind was from the north. The weather was overcast just after a heavy rain that morning. I was using a Marryat MR8A fly reel with an 8½' Browning Diana 7 weight rod with a ten-pound test Cabela's bonefish leader.

On August 29, 2004, I caught fish 59 in Lake Humphreys near Marlow, Oklahoma. She was a common carp measuring 23" and weighing five pounds, and took a #10 bead head Prince Nymph. I was wading the flats just left of the boat ramp and sight-casting toward a tailing carp who was making a mud puff. The weather was mostly sunny, with temperatures in the mideighties and a light southeast wind. The water was brown stained but semiclear. I was using a 6 ½' Wright & McGill Eagle Claw Featherlight 5 weight rod with a Martin Classic MC56 reel and a ten-pound tippet.

My last entry in this volume is fish 94, a flathead catfish caught on July 28, 2012, using a #3/0 orange-and-white Pistol Pete I tied primarily for bass. This fish measured 17½" and was caught from my Hobie Cat kick boat while fishing along the riprap on the south side of the Oklahoma City Boat Club boat docks in Lake Hefner in Oklahoma City. My records say that it was in the middle of a heat wave of consecutive one-hundred-degree-plus days. The temperature was ninety degrees but getting hot rapidly at 7:00 a.m. when the fish hit. There was no wind.

Examples of Things You Can Do with Your Data

<u>Bass Stomach Contents Log</u> (From the early days before catch-and-release!)

1.	Empty	25
2.	Green sunfish	13
3.	Crayfish	6
4.	Largemouth bass	4
5.	Unidentified fish	4

6.	Bullfrog	2
7.	Bluegill	2
8.	Turtle	2
9.	Shad	1
10.	White Bass	1
11.	Plastic Worm	1
12.	Snails	1

Bass by Month (1963-2019)—A nearly perfect bell curve!

January	5
February	20
March	30
April	62
May	106
June	160
July	112
August	87
September	62
October	40
November	7
December	5

Earliest and Latest Bass Catches by Type of Artificial Bait (1963-2019)

Bait	Earliest	Latest
Spoon	January 21	October 19
Plastic worm	March 29	November 29
Topwater	May 17	September 29
Crank bait	February 4	November 10

Spinnerbait	January 24	December 27
Fly pattern—surface	May 26	September 30
Fly pattern—subsurface	February 2	December 8
Fly pattern—deep	February 20	November 5

Bass by Wind Direction (1963-2019)

1. No Wind   151
2. South   136
3. Southeast   111
4. Southwest   64
5. North   49
6. Northeast   49
7. East   35
8. West   28
9. Northwest   25

So much for Uncle Chuck's fishing postulate (at least regarding a west wind)!

When the Wind is from the west, that's when fishing is best.
When the wind is from the south, it blows the lure into the fish's mouth.
When the wind is from the east, that's when fishing is least.
When the wind is from the north, thou shalt not go forth.

CHAPTER FIVE

JOURNALING MY MOST GRATIFYING FISH

Once I began fly-fishing exclusively, I noticed that I kept hearing many of the same comments from my friends, acquaintances, and other fishermen—comments like "Fly-fishing looks like it would be fun, but I like to catch bigger fish," "Yep, bluegill fishing is a lot of fun, but I'm a bass fisherman," "Where do you fly fish around here?" "I'm a spinnerbait guy," "Sometimes you really have to go deep to catch bass," "I like to go after catfish," and "I like to fish saltwater." While well intentioned and not designed to offend me and my new angling pursuit, these comments nonetheless really let me know how many misconceptions there were about fly-fishing. So partly in an attempt to prove them wrong, and partly because it sounded like something fun and challenging to do, I decided to develop a new journal dedicated to logging fish of all species, similar to what I had done the past thirty years exclusively for bass. My new mission statement would be "If it has gills, swims, and eats, it's fair game!" About that same time, I discovered the website www.flyanglersonline.com and noticed that its message board had an entire section dedicated to warm-water fly-fishing and that fly anglers from all over the country were as dedicated to carp and catfish as they were to trout and salmon. Man, was this going to be fun!

I also realized that my definition of a log-worthy fish would have to be redefined. For me it was easy to make the cutoff for bass at 1½ pounds, because this size of fish can give you quite a battle and are not that easy to catch. But what about species like green sunfish, crappies, drum, bullheads, suckers, etc.? What constitutes a quality fish for these species? Trout Unlimited, in their publication *Trout Magazine*, will typically ask the person they are recognizing as a "Stream Champion" what his or her "Most Memorable Fish" was. For me, the log I developed is more than a recognition of my most memorable fish; it's more of an honor roll of gratifying fish. Thus, I came up with the concept of a "gratifying fish." In developing the criteria for this new journal, it was important for me to understand that there are a number of factors that go into determining what makes the pursuit and landing of any given fish such a wonderful experience that it should be logged and included on this list. And while the size of the fish is always a key factor, it is not necessarily the most important thing. Some examples might include a fish that is rare or protected (e.g., a bull trout); a fish that is extremely difficult to catch on a fly pattern (e.g., flathead catfish); a fish from a fishery that historically, for whatever reason, has not been productive for me (e.g., Lake Overholser in Oklahoma City); a new or unique fishery experience (e.g., saltwater flats); a unique fishing method (e.g., Tenkara); a fish taken on a fly pattern that I personally designed and tied (e.g., a Ginger Bugger); a fish caught on a vintage bamboo fly rod that I personally refurbished (e.g., a beaten-up South Bend rod); a fish caught in inclement weather (e.g., a sleet storm); and a fish caught under extremely difficult circumstances (e.g., on a broken leg). All of these are actual examples that are represented on my "Most Gratifying Fish" list. Christopher Camuto, contributing writer to *Trout Magazine* probably summed it up best when he made the comment "So much of the pleasure of angling is triggered by our chance to respond, in temperament and tactic to the conditions we find ourselves in." It's not easy to make this list, as there have been some years in which no selections were made at all. The most entries made in a single year were seven, and that happened only one time. Some fish on this list do not represent the largest I've ever caught of particular species but rather represent a unique set of circumstances that, when put altogether, caused me to just sit back after the catch, reflect on what just happened, and then feel my internal battery being recharged as I quietly said to myself, "Ahh, this feels really good!"

At this book's writing, I've recognized seventy-three fish in the order of how gratifying the catch was to me personally, along with specific narratives detailing the circumstances surrounding the experience that made them special. Twenty-nine different species are represented on that list. Rather than include all seventy-three fish in this chapter, I've chosen to highlight the top twenty from those seventy-three to give the reader an idea of all the factors that went into making them fish I would never forget. What's interesting is that I still remember every one of them as though they were landed just yesterday. Some of that is probably because I often refer to this particular journal during the cold winter months to revisit each special experience. It's so nice to know that I have them on record in the most favorite of all my journals, the one that recognizes the most gratifying of all the fish I've caught on a fly rod. From that journal, here's the top twenty:

JOURNAL OF MY 20 MOST GRATIFYING FISH ON A FLY ROD

1. **39" Northern Pike, caught in Black Sturgeon Lake, Ontario, Canada, 5/30/95, on a #2 Whitlock's Deep Sheep Sunfish using a 9' Cabela's St. John's 8/9 weight rod with a Cabela's 789 reel**

I had just started my journey into the world of fly-fishing, and this was my first major fishing trip with the long rod on my annual excursion to Canada with buddies (Bruce Gray, Jim Smith, Don Duckwall, and Bob Verboon). I took my share of good-natured ribbing all week about the "swish-swish" sound coming from the constant back-and-forward casts, but I finally got some respect when I caught the trip fish using a full-sink line and a Whitlock's Deep Sheep Sunfish on Black Sturgeon Lake. The other two boats gathered up close to watch me land the monster. Fortunately, I have most of the fight on video. With dimensions of thirty-nine by seventeen inches, it came to 14½ lbs. Later that season, it was gratifying to receive in the mail the annual Crawford's Resort newsletter from Nestor Falls, where we stayed, and see that the fish was highlighted as one of the largest pike caught that year, with the special side note "and on a fly rod."

2. <u>**20" Brown Trout**</u>, **caught in the Alumine River, Patagonia, Argentina, 2/1/06, on a #6 cone head black Woolly Bugger using a DAM Black Panther 7/8 weight 9'3" rod with a Ross Cimarron C1 reel**

The fly-fishing group that is organized by Ron Perry and affectionately referred to as the Royal Wulff Society took our most exotic trip yet—an excursion to Argentina, where local guides instructed us on their tried and tested methods using local patterns and strategies for rainbows. Following shore lunches each day, a number of us would venture out on our own while our guides were taking their siestas. It was on one such venture that I landed the trip fish, as well as the only two browns caught on the entire trip, when I found a deep cove that I had to hike down to with my DAM telescoping rod rigged with Teeny T-200 sinking-head line. I caught two Browns (eighteen inches and twenty inches) on a cone head black Woolly Bugger. The guides at first didn't believe that I'd caught a brown and accused me of catching two of their local native rough fish until they saw the proof represented by a visual image of photo taken by Don Humphries on his digital camera, who had been fishing nearby and made the hike to the honey hole I discovered.

3.   <u>22" Rainbow Trout</u>, caught in the Red River, New Mexico, 9/29/17, on a #8 Ginger Bugger using a 6' bamboo midge rod with a vintage Heddon 300 reel

On our annual fall trip to New Mexico, I typically rig up a small fly rod and keep it in the cabin specifically for fishing the stretch of river that runs next to us. This time I rigged my six-foot bamboo rod with a vintage Heddon reel and DT3F line for the small eight to ten-inch fish we usually catch in that part of the river. I was fishing the last hole on the last day of a frustrating trip after having landed only two fish in three days of fishing the Red River, Rio Costilla, and Eagle Nest Lake. My back was hurting, and I had given up, but my son Jim convinced me to fish with him around the cabin some before we began packing for the trip home, and am I ever glad he did. In the hole about forty yards upriver from the cabin, I hooked a broad-shouldered twenty-two-by-fourteen-inch monster rainbow who came from out of nowhere to nail my Ginger Bugger, putting all kinds of stress on my little bamboo rod and four-pound-test tippet. It was fun to listen to the decades-old click-and-pawl drag sing on every run she made toward the falls. The fish weighed 5.39 pounds, making her the biggest trout I ever caught. But the best thing about it was that Jim was there standing beside me to see every second of the battle, from the take to netting it for me, and he even got some great video of the struggle using his smartphone. This was a very special moment shared with my son!

4. <u>28" Channel Catfish</u>, caught in Homestead Lake, Edmond, Oklahoma, 7/1/04, on a #2 orange and lime Wooly Bugger using a refurbished 8½' South Bend 55-9 bamboo rod with a vintage Herters 709 reel

John Sievert had been telling me about a residential lake near his house in Edmond that had a good population of grass carp and giant bluegill. I thought it would be a good time to test the nine-foot South Bend bamboo fly rod I had just refurbished after purchasing it on eBay. Thinking I might be able to see how it handled some feisty bluegills, I put on my favorite orange and lime Woolly Bugger that I had tied especially for Dad's pond. On one of the farthest casts I made all night straight toward the middle of the pond—*boom!*—the big cat hit it immediately on the surface like a bass, and the fight was on. With a limber rod and four-pound-test tippet, there wasn't much I could do except hold on and hope she stayed deep and away from any underwater obstructions. With dimensions of twenty-eight by fifteen inches, its weight was calculated at 8 lbs. 7 oz. It was beginning to get dark as a gallery developed in the neighborhood before I finally managed to wear her down enough to land her, take a photo, and release her.

5. <u>24" Brown Trout</u>, caught in the White River, Arkansas, 10/20/18, on a #6 bead head brown Girdle Bug using a 9' Sage RPL+ 5 weight rod with a Sougayilang reel

After some miserable but fairly productive fishing in rainy forty-five-degree weather the day before below the Bull Shoals dam, the sun came out and the temperature reached a comfortable seventy degrees. Jerry Hocker and I fished with a great guide, Kevin Brandtonies, who had convinced us to leave the dam and fish a crowded stretch of river near the Cotter Bridge. Jerry and I caught over twenty rainbows in the twelve to fourteen-inch range despite all the traffic. Then, on a midafternoon run downriver, I set the hook on what seemed to be a routine take of my Girdle Bug, and wow! It was anything but routine, as this huge twenty-four-inch brown immediately let me know she would be a force to be reckoned with. She fought hard and slow, and stayed deep, constantly letting me feel her powerful head shakes on my sensitive Sage fly rod. Eventually I gained enough ground to see my strike indicator again and nearly lost my breath when I saw how big she was. At two feet and 5.7 lbs., she was by far my largest brown trout ever and easily the trip fish of a group of mostly spin fishermen. A photo of me with this special fish was later featured in *Dally's Ozark Fly Fisher*, an online magazine. What a special fish this was—one I will never forget!

6. **19" Brown Trout**, **caught in the Rio Grande, New Mexico, 9/30/98, on a #8 black and chartreuse $\frac{1}{64}$ oz. marabou jig using an 8½' St. Croix Pro Graphite 5/6 weight rod with a Martin Classic MC 56 reel**

This was a solo trip to the cabin at Red River, New Mexico, to contemplate life following my pending divorce. After spending some time exploring all parts of the Red River, I went to Starr Angler Fly Shop and asked for advice on new fishing areas. There I got directions on how to get to the John Dunn Bridge on the banks of the Rio Grande. At this time in my fly-fishing journey, brown trout were the real elusive gem of the salmonid family, and to catch this size fish when the average trout ranged from ten to twelve inches was a real prize and really elevated my confidence in exploring new and bigger water and going after new species of fish. I caught the fish on a black and yellow marabou jig that I had purchased many, many years ago from the Roaring River Lodge Store in Cassville, Missouri, back in the sixties during a family vacation.

7. <u>21½" Red Drum</u>, caught off Mustang Island Road, Port
   Aransas, Texas, 4/12/00, on a #1 orange and chartreuse
   Clouser Deep Minnow using an 8 ½' Browning Diana 7
   weight rod with a Marryat MR8A reel

My good friend Bob Verboon and I drove down to Port Aransas,
Texas, in his new diesel Dodge Ram to test our freshwater fly-
fishing skills on redfish (red drum). Neither of us had ever done
any saltwater fly-fishing, so we had a guide hired the day after we
arrived. Eager just to get out and do some saltwater flats fishing,
we asked a local merchant where a good place to fish might be,
and she directed us to Mustang Island. Having no idea what
we were doing, we drove up to a likely-looking spot and began
wading the area. I noticed some disturbance on one shoreline and
put on an orange and chartreuse Clouser Deep Minnow that I
had tied for bass back home. To my surprise, I caught the trip's
only fish—a healthy redfish that pleased me beyond measure.
The next day, with a professional guide and a boat, we fished all
day and never saw a single fish, which made this fish even more
special.

8. <u>21" Rainbow Trout</u>, caught in the Lower Mountain Fork
   River, Oklahoma, 11/8/03, on a #12 brown PH Nymph
   using an 8' Browning Diana 4 weight rod with a Ross
   Cimarron C1 reel

This fish was caught during a fishing trip with Jim, A. B., and
Tom Adams to the Lower Mountain Fork River. The day before,
Jim caught a pickerel in Eagle Creek, which was the first one I
had ever seen. The second day, we fished the Mountain Fork with
Jim and Tom Adams going one direction and A. B. and I going
another. I was dead drifting a specially tied brown bead head
nymph I had designed that was made primarily with natural

human hair. I found a great-looking hole and cast the nymph a few times before two kayakers went right through the middle of my drift. Frustrated by their inconsideration, I let the hole rest a while. When I returned, the big 'bow took my strike indicator down with authority. Immediately I knew I had something special on, and I had to walk down the river twenty to thirty yards to keep her from breaking off. Photos of this fish were displayed at both Backwoods outfitters in Oklahoma City and in the Three Rivers Fly Shop outside Broken Bow, Oklahoma.

9. <u>19" Cutthroat Trout</u>, **caught in Hossick Lake, Colorado, 8/15/96, on a #12 gold bead Super Worm using an 8' White River Dogwood Canyon 6 weight rod with a Cabela's 789 reel**

This fish was caught following a thirteen-and-a-half-hour backpacking trip to Hossick Lake in the Weminuche Wilderness area in Colorado, near Pagosa Springs. Jim, Bob Verboon, and I, along with some guys from the State Career and Technology Department, made the grueling hike, which was seven miles and took us a day and a half. The alpine lake was well above the tree line, and we struggled for a while before Jim began to catch some fish on the second day. I'll never forget Jim waking me up from a nap in my tent, shouting, "Dad! Dad!"—a sure sign he had a nice one on. With renewed confidence, I went back out and caught this big cut, which was the trip fish and was caught on a nymph pattern called a gold bead head Super Worm I had purchased in a Tulsa fly shop while I was at the Career-Tech Summer Conference. I later entered a photo of the fish in the North American Fishing Club's annual Catch & Release Contest and won the first-place prize in the cutthroat division. The first-place prize was a replica of the fish, which I now have hanging in the man cave. I also had my picture published along with those of the other winners in their magazine, *North American Fisherman.*

10. <u>**17" Smallmouth Bass,**</u> **caught in Pennington Creek, Oklahoma, 4/25/98, on a #2 orange and chartreuse Road Runner Bucktail Streamer using an 8 ½' St. Croix Pro Graphite 5/6 weight rod with a Martin Classic MC 56 reel**

Jim and I met A. B. in Pauls Valley and then loaded up my Jeep Grand Cherokee and drove to Pennington Creek to fish for smallmouth bass. Jim and A. B. had both fished Pennington before, but this was my first trip there. The average size is typically in the ten to twelve-inch range, but this big boy struck in shallow water and made a run right at me downriver, spinning me around a complete 180 degrees. It was the trip fish and was quite a prize for such a small creek. Like brown trout are to rainbows, I've always felt smallmouth are more valued than largemouth, which made it even sweeter. I caught the fish on a special fly I tied and designed that features a small swivel and willow leaf blade that is connected with JB Weld to the hook near the eye. I call it a Road Runner Bucktail Streamer because the spinning blade is attached underneath, in a similar fashion to the way the conventional Road Runner lures are designed.

11. <u>**15" Bull Trout,**</u> **caught in the Selway River, Idaho, 6/24/10 on a #4 yellow Dan Delekta's Delektable Screamer using an 8' White River Dogwood Canyon 6 weight rod with a Ross Cimarron C1 reel**

This was one of Ron Perry's fishing trips. We flew into Missoula, Montana, and then rode a yellow bus for two hours into Idaho to launch five white-water rafts for a four-night, five-day, forty-seven-mile float trip down the Selway, which we were told held only native fish. I really wanted to catch a bull trout, which was endangered, and during a brief visit to a local fly shop, I asked what patterns bulls were most likely to hit on the Selway. The guy at the shop suggested a big #4 cone-headed yellow streamer called a Delektable Screamer. After catching numerous very small wild native cuts on dry flies, we camped at a great-looking spot where some massive white water flowed into a large slower pool. I was the only fly angler who had brought a sinking-head line, and I used that outfit with the big yellow streamer using a slow strip after the flow took it downriver, and then *bam!* On the fourth cast, the bully hit it, and a crowd gathered immediately to watch me bring her in. This was by far the largest fish of the trip and the only bull trout caught. I was a little bit embarrassed by the way I screamed when I knew what I had on. It was indeed a dream come true on this trip. A beautiful and rare fish.

12. **<u>19" Brown Trout</u>, caught in the Lower Mountain Fork River, Oklahoma, 4/30/10, on a #10 Ginger Bugger using an 8½' St. Croix 5/6 weight rod with a Ross Cimarron C1 reel**

Jim and I were fishing below the reregulation dam of the Mountain Fork River as part of the Annual St. Paul's Flyfishers of Men trip. We probably had the best day fishing together ever! On this single day, Jim caught two big browns (eighteen inches and twenty inches), and I caught this dandy nineteen incher, all on a fly I designed and tied myself—a jig-head ginger woolly bugger using wool for the body instead of chenille and with an extra-long marabou tail. What a great feeling! I've had success with this fly nearly everywhere I've used it, from the Rio Grande to Yellowstone. Jim also caught a nineteen-inch rainbow in the Evening Hole area the day before on the exact same pattern. The fly seems to match tan-colored sculpins, which are everywhere throughout the Lower Mountain Fork. The guys on the trip also had a little local contest going in three categories, and Jim won two of the three, so he took back a little money to boot! Great trip!

13. **21" Rainbow Trout, caught in the Red River, New Mexico, 10/6/94, on a #10 renegade pattern Pistol Pete using a 5' South Bend midge rod with a vintage Weber Weberkraft 500 reel**

Bruce Gray and his wife Pat went with Jo and me to our cabin in Red River, New Mexico, for a family vacation. Of course, Bruce and I were going to sneak off for a little fishing in between the sightseeing. Just eighty paces upriver from our cabin, there was a good-sized hole where we had seen some large trout earlier. This was before the monster Canada pike that I was yet to catch the following year, so Bruce was still not convinced that fly-fishing gear was adequate for decent-sized fish. While everyone was taking an afternoon nap in the cabin, I walked over to the hole, and to my shock and amazement, this huge 'bow came out of the deep to suck up my Pistol Pete. This was a huge confidence builder for me and was a monster trout by Red River standards. Bruce, never to be outdone, went the following day during a brief rainstorm and caught a twenty-four incher in the same hole! Of course, he cheated, using an ultralight spinning outfit with a Super Duper lure! We had both fish mounted together, and they are currently hanging above the fireplace in our Red River cabin.

14. **19" Largemouth Bass, caught in a Payne County farm pond, Oklahoma, 9/3/94, on a #2 olive Hank Roberts Hair Worm using a 9' Cabela's St. John's 8/9 weight rod with a Cabela's 789 reel**

I was still new to the sport of angling for bass with a fly rod, and this fish added tremendous confidence in my pursuit of warm-water fly-fishing. I drove to Uncle Bert's farm, parked my Jeep Cherokee next to his house, and walked through the pasture to the smaller of his two farm ponds. This pond was always clear, and I could nearly cast across it, but it had always produced an amazing number of large bass for its size. At nearly the end of my retrieve, the bass just exploded on the shoreline near my feet on an olive Hank Roberts Hair Worm. I was so excited to catch a lunker bass on a fly. I regretted not having a camera with me to memorialize this major milestone with a photo before I released her.

15. **20" Common Carp, caught in Taylor Lake, Oklahoma, 7/17/04, on a #12 bead head Prince Nymph using an 8½' St. Croix Pro Graphite 5/6 weight rod with an Orvis Clearwater III reel**

I had been corresponding with two fly-fishers, Robert McMahan from Altus and John Sievert from Edmond, whom I met online on the bulletin board of www.flyanglersonline.com (FAOL). After several weeks of correspondence, the three of us first met for a fishing trip to American Horse Lake in Geary. After realizing that we were extremely compatible, we decided to schedule another trip to Taylor Lake, just outside Rush Springs, after learning that a study conducted by the Oklahoma Department of Wildlife Conservation showed this lake to have the largest quality bass population per acre of water surface. After an unsuccessful attempt of pursuing largemouth bass, John, who had always talked about how much fun carp were on a fly rod, noticed that there were several cruisers in the flats surrounding most of the lake. I had never caught a carp on a fly and had always wanted to learn the sport. After both Robert (who was also a carp virgin) and John had landed some nice carp, it seemed like forever before I finally enticed my first carp to turn and suck up a bead head

Prince Nymph. Since that time, I have caught many carp that were larger than this one, but because of the uniqueness of this challenge (sight fishing) and the difficulty I had in learning the skill, this catch has to rank right up there as a monumental first in my fly-fishing journey.

16. <u>11" Bluegill Sunfish</u>, **caught in a Payne County farm pond, Oklahoma, 5/10/94, on a #8 black and gray Woolly Bugger using a Cabela's St. John's 8/9 weight 9' rod with a Cabela's 789 reel**

I was still learning how to fly fish and tie flies when I took the short walk from my house to Dad's pond. I had just tied a black and gray Woolly Bugger from the instructional video I ordered from Bass Pro and thought I'd give it a try. The fish hit hard, and I recall after a couple of significant boils that this fish (a bass?) was fighting kind of strangely. Then, on a final boil near the surface, I saw a bright yellow flash and realized that it wasn't a bass at all! This was by far the largest bluegill I had ever caught. I was alone and had no camera, so I put it on a stringer and quickly drove to Dad's house to show it off. Jim happened to be there visiting the folks and luckily had a camera and promptly took a photo. Dad was so impressed with her size that he didn't want to kill and clean her, so I revived her in the stock tank and drove her back to the pond, where I released her in fine shape. Not only was this the largest bluegill that I had ever caught, but it was the catch that gave me confidence in my fly-tying ability. I now knew that I could tie a pattern good enough to fool a big fish.

17. <u>17 ¼" Black Crappie</u>, **caught in the Francis Tuttle west pond, Oklahoma City, 4/20/19, on a #8 tungsten bead head Golden Woolly Bugger Mega Worm using a 9' Fenwick HMG 10 weight rod with an Aikelen ZF-85 reel**

A. B. and I had been catching some really nice crappie in the fifteen-inch range in Francis Tuttle's west pond over the past two weeks and went again today to see if the magic was still there. We arrived around 1:00 p.m. and had little success until 3:40 p.m., when this 17¼" monster hit a pattern A. B. had designed and tied for me, which is basically a gold-colored Woolly Bugger tied on a jig hook using a gold tungsten bead with a cream mega worm as the tail. According to internet charts, this fish weighed 3½ pounds. It fought like a big bass, which is what I thought I had on until I was finally able to get it to shore. It was the biggest crappie I had ever seen! What a special fish in the unlikeliest of urban ponds.

18. <u>**19" Smallmouth Bass**</u>, **caught in Lake Obabikon, Ontario, Canada, 6/5/03, on a #3/0 white Noisy Popper using a 9' Cabela's St. John's 8/9 weight rod with a Martin M6 reel**

This fish was very stocky (probably full of eggs) and should have been one of two smallies that made the gratifying list on this trip, but my net man didn't follow my instructions on how to net the fish, and she got off when he hit her midbody with the rim of the net as he tried to lift her into the boat. That particular fish hit a Crease Fly and was even larger, and was thoroughly played out, which made losing her even more painful. So this nineteen-inch fish was a kind of consolation prize. Getting her into the net helped ease the sting of that earlier disappointment, as it was still, by far, my largest smallmouth on a fly rod. The smallmouth bass were really active on top on Lake Obabikon in Ontario, which certainly played to the strengths of a fly rod. I caught her on a large white bass popper that I had purchased as part of an assortment from a guy who made them and was offering them through an auction on eBay. They are very unique, having a built-in rattle and large eyes, and being very rough looking and reeking with the smell of tobacco, which may add to their fish appeal. I have used them effectively back home for largemouths. No name was given by the maker, so when someone asks what I'm using, I refer to it as an eBay noisy popper.

19. <u>**21" Largemouth Bass,**</u> **caught in a Payne County farm pond, Oklahoma, 5/23/98 on a #4 orange and blue Woolly Bugger using an 8'4" Orvis Power Matrix 3 weight rod with an ATH Gallatin 1 reel**

This fish was extremely rewarding because I was using a pattern I had tied specifically for bluegills and was trying out my new 3 weight Orvis rod and ATH Reel, thinking I'd have some fun with a light outfit on the big bluegills that I'd been catching recently in Dad's pond. This was my first lunker bass from Dad's pond, and it took me by complete surprise, engulfing the small orange and blue Woolly Bugger and then taking off for deep water. Fortunately, at the time, there wasn't a lot of brush in Dad's pond; if there had been, I seriously doubt I could have steered her away from hanging up on something with such a light rig. Big bass have been hard to come by for me on a fly rod, so this was doubly gratifying because it was so unexpected.

20. <u>**19" Largemouth Bass,**</u> **caught in a Payne County farm pond, Oklahoma, 3/17/16, on a #2 orange and silver Pistol Pete using a 9' Fenwick HMG 10 weight rod with an Aikelen ZF-85 reel**

It was spring break, and I took the day off to visit Mom and get some fishing in at the family farm pond before a cold front was to hit the next day. It was a perfect early spring day, mostly sunny, with a light east wind and seventy-two degrees. Measuring in at a length of nineteen inches and a girth of fourteen inches, this may have been my heaviest largemouth yet on a fly rod. Using multiple calculators found on the internet, I estimated her weight to be somewhere between 4.25 and 4.65 pounds, based on those dimensions. I didn't weigh her with a scale because I didn't want to stress her any more than possible, as she was obviously full of eggs. She was one of the fattest bass I'd seen in years, and I was amazed by her girth. Despite her obesity, she was a very healthy specimen and fought hard and deep, almost like a catfish. I caught her on a #2 orange-and-silver Pistol Pete using my Fenwick 10 weight rig. This was my first lunker bass on a fly rod since 2003, so you can imagine the joy in my heart after such a long dry spell of lunkerless bass seasons.

CHAPTER SIX
BE A STORYTELLER

When I was a little boy, there were occasions when I thought a good way to keep from getting into trouble, would be to tell a little fib, and my mom would always see right through me and say, "Now, Tommy, are you telling me a story?" When I heard those words, I immediately knew that it would be in my best interest to come clean, and the truth would always be blurted out. Of course, fishermen are notorious for telling little fibs of all sizes when it comes to describing their fishing prowess. This tendency to perhaps be a little loose with the truth was once noted by Ed Zern, who in 1945 boldly hypothesized that "all fishermen are born honest, but they get over it."

So your assumption at this point, based on the title of this chapter, might easily be that I'm going to focus on how to tell convincing exaggerated stories about successes or near misses that really never happened. And while acquiring that skill might add some value to your fishing pleasure, this chapter is instead about the creative art of describing your experiences on the water, either on paper or in the spoken voice, so that it is of considerable interest to others as well as yourself.

I've recently become a fan of Christopher Camuto, writer for *Trout Magazine*, and have added him to my list of all-time favorite outdoor writers. I view him as a key influencer on my philosophy regarding the importance of fishing. In his article featured in the summer 2007 edition, he focuses on storytelling as it relates to family and fishing, centering his story on the book *Early Northwest Fly-Fishing: A Fly Angler's Lifetime Journey Through Oregon, Washington and the World*. The book is based on the journaling of Blake Hallock. The impetus for putting that book together, came about when one of Hallock's daughters discovered journals accounting of her father's fishing experiences dating back to the 1880s.   Camuto goes on in his article to warn us that "usually the discovery of journals and type-scripts in attics and basements turns out to be of interest only to family members. But in this case, however, the typescript was a find and a lifetime of fishing stories—one man's stream of consciousness— was rescued from oblivion by a handful of thoughtful people." I'm not going to go anywhere close to presuming that my fifty-six years of journaling will come anywhere near to having Hallock's level of significance, but the point I think Camuto is trying to make, and one that I would like to expound upon, is that the connection to family that our beloved sport can have ties us to something that transcends our short life on this precious planet. Typically, fishing stories live only one or maybe two generations before they are lost for future generations to enjoy. That doesn't have to be the case if you journal. Camuto seems to drive that point home when he says later in his article, "In narrative a moment fishing with your father can meld into another decades later, fishing with your son. Telling a story, you see how your daughter's casting motion mimics your wife's, and understand the similarity in their echoing laugh when a fly comes free from a missed fish. Maybe, the fishing's not done until the story is told."

Journaling goes hand-in-glove with storytelling, which, according to Peter Guber of the *Harvard Business Review*, "can be traced back thousands of years to the days of the shaman around the tribal fire who would record the oral history, its triumphs and tragedies." Ursula K. Le Guin expands on that notion with her thoughts: "The story—from *Rumpelstiltskin* to *War and Peace*—is one of the basic tools invented by the human mind for the purpose of understanding. There have been great societies that did not use the wheel, but there have been no societies that did not tell stories." And finally, Max DePree, in his book *Leadership Is an Art*, makes a strong case for storytelling when he says, "Every family, every college, every corporation, every institution needs tribal storytellers. The penalty for failing to listen is to lose one's history, one's historical context, one's binding values."

So what do tribal fishing stories look like, and which ones are worthy of recording for the enjoyment of future generations? Well, that depends on the values of the person doing the journaling and will vary widely as to what is and is not important to be repeated in narrative. What follows is a small sampling of my personal fishing experiences that I hope to keep in our family for generations to come.

One of the smartest things I ever did was put a fishing rod in the hands of my son Jim when he was barely old enough to walk. Zebco, at one time, made a starter spincasting reel called a ZeeBee. Teamed with a five-foot glass rod, it made the perfect rig for a four-year-old. On a family vacation to the Arkansas Ozarks, my first wife and I took Jim to a trout farm where visitors paid by the pound for hungry rainbow meat swimming in the water. I have some wonderful Super 8 home movies of Jim, his little biceps straining, bringing in one rainbow after another until we finally had to say enough because we were afraid there wouldn't be any money left to buy gas for the trip home. In my mind, that was the day our boy became a fisherman. A young child needs to experience success early in his or her fishing journey to get addicted to the thrill of a pole bending beyond reason. As they say, "The tug is the drug," and my son was hooked from that day forward.

My son Jim proudly holding up his first rainbow trout.

As Jim grew, so did his trout.

Later, as Jim grew older, we went on many other fishing adventures together. One of the most memorable trips was the time we scouted some range management ponds the park rangers used to reduce overgrazing by bison, elk, and longhorn cattle located in the Wichita Mountains Wildlife Refuge near Lawton, Oklahoma. After purchasing a topographic map at the visitor center, we located some small ponds and began the long hike to scout them out. Following a two-mile hike, we found one pond that had rarely been fished; this was obvious because of all the stunted ten to twelve-inch bass we were catching with relative ease and a minimum of applied skill. Then Jim, who was twelve years old at the time, and I saw something strange come out from the depths of the pond that, when it surfaced, acted like a giant buzzbait as it quickly and erratically began heading straight toward Jim. In a panic, I screamed at Jim some words that I'll remember the rest of my life: "Jim, I don't know what that is, but we'd better get out of its way right now!" Just about that time, it suddenly disappeared. I am very reluctant to even mention this incident for fear that it may detract from any creditability I might have with the reader. But it happened, and I have my son as a witness who still talks about that incident to this day.

Now, just for the sake of discussion, and one possibility that has helped me throughout the years to come to grips with that wild story, is that the area we were fishing in the refuge bordered restricted land owned by the Fort Sill Army Training Center. So maybe it had something to do with a top army secret—maybe an experimental unidentified submersible object (USO) of some sort. I'm still in hopes that whatever it was will soon be declassified so I can begin telling the story to others without fear of people thinking I'm a fruitcake. I feel so weird even telling this story because I am always quick to make fun of people who claim to have seen Bigfoot or the Loch Ness monster. And no, I don't have a fuzzy picture of it that I am offering as proof that it existed. But that incident was the type that bonds you to whoever you're with at the time, and in this case it was my son, which only serves to make it even more special. Since that time, Jim and I have taken many fishing trips together and shared many experiences on the water, watching each other catch and lose fish, as well as serving as chief photographers and trusted net men for each other's prize catches. Jim has been a wonderful source of joy for me and is truly my best friend. Only twenty years separates us in age, so in some ways I feel as if he's my younger brother. But in a bit of a role reversal, and because he is such a wise and mature person well beyond his years that I look up to in so many ways, I often tell other people when describing my son that he is my role model and that someday, when I grow up, I want to be just like him. It's truly how I feel about him, and I hope that it eventually happens.

I am also fortunate to have an older cousin who is also more like a brother to me than a cousin. He was my role model growing up and my very first fishing buddy. A. B. is actually a double cousin. Now, for those of you unfamiliar with the term "double cousin," let me explain. Both my parents are first-generation born-in-America German Lutherans, which probably led to some interesting features that most families probably can't identify with. My dad, Adolph, married my mother, Florence Voise. And my dad's two brothers, Bert and Gus, married my mother's two sisters, Sophie and Lillian. So in my family, we had three brothers marrying three sisters, which meant I had a bunch of cousins that I was related to on both sides of the family (i.e., double cousins). And just for good measure, some of Dad's cousins also married some of mom's cousins, making the Voise–Friedemann bond even closer. Almost sounds illegal, doesn't it? But I checked all the laws, and everything is legit. But it was a lot of fun for us cousins during the holidays when we would all see each other, regardless of whether it was the Friedemann or Voise side of the family. I think what happened was that one German Lutheran family found another German Lutheran family in nearby Perry, Oklahoma, just thirty miles away from Stillwater, and it just seemed to make a lot of sense to join the two families in an effort to eliminate much of the adjustment that sometimes occurs when marrying outside faith and culture.

A German Lutheran Legacy - three Friedemann brothers marry three Voise sisters. My parents Adolph and Florence are on the left. A.B.'s parents Bert and Lillian, are on the right. Gus and Sophia are in the middle.

So, having explained all that double-cousin stuff, let's get back to double cousin A. B., because he was the one who really developed my love for fishing and was every bit as passionate about the sport as I eventually became. Being seven years older and living only a mile from me on his dad's farm, he would always drag me along with him to fish the multitude of farm ponds we had within a five-mile radius of both our farms. In fact, he was the one who first told me about Sam Welch and journaling, and he began writing his own journals in 1959, four years before I started mine in 1963. We've had some marvelous times fishing together, and I cannot ever remember a cross word between us.

Being older, A. B. was the one who could legally drive, and we would take his father's 1948 Willys Jeep pickup truck to our fishing ponds. Several times during the spring rains, we would get stuck and have to walk to the nearest farmhouse to call one of our parents for help, which always meant getting the tractor and pulling us out of the mud and muck. I always hated going to Cecil Jones's pond, because we had to negotiate a low spot in the trail that was always muddy, and I remember A. B. stopping about fifty feet from the mud hole and then flooring the Jeep to hopefully speed us through the mud before we got stuck. Sometimes it worked, and sometimes it didn't. On our smarter days, we would take his dad's Ford 8N tractor, and I would ride on the fender with my tackle box in one hand and a rod in the other hand, trying to keep my balance so I wouldn't fall off. That all seems hard to imagine in today's society, with mandatory seat belts, buckled-down child seats, airbags, etc. But we always had a great time fishing with each other, and I learned as much just by watching him as I did from reading outdoor magazines and books about fishing. It was like getting the theory in classroom by reading about it at home and then watching A. B. put all that theory to use at the pond.

Cousin A.B. with a prize bass in front of the Willys Jeep
pickup that took us to farm ponds all over Payne County.

We also had a unique way of increasing our access to additional
farm ponds. Back then, every time a farmer would build a new
pond for his livestock, one of us would go to the farmer's house
and ask him if we could stock it for him with bluegill, bass, and
crappie. We usually got an enthusiastic yes, as well as permission
to fish the pond whenever we wanted. While it was certainly a
self-serving offer, it was the first time that I learned about win-
win deals and how establishing mutually beneficial partnerships
could get me ahead in life—a skill that I would later use many
times as a CEO in my professional life as an adult. People who
are able to master that skill truly live by the principle that their
net worth is their network, and I attribute my acquisition of that
talent back to those early days when I was just trying to get more
places to fish.

By the way, A. B. and I were quite successful in stocking those
ponds with fish from other productive farm ponds. They were

naturally marked because of the hole we would often stab in the soft part of the lower jaw when attaching them to the stringer, and we often caught the same bass later in the season with that hole exposed. And because the fish came from multiple farm ponds, we theorized that the gene pool was improved, giving us a better breed of fish in every species we stocked. I was amazed at how long a bass, crappie, or bluegill could survive in a five-gallon bucket of nonaerated water as we transported it from one pond to another in the back of a pickup truck or sometimes in the basket of a bicycle. Sometimes when a pond was mud-stained and had poor water clarity, we would take our dad's pickups into town and take Sheetrock scraps from home building sites to various farm ponds to help clear them up. It always worked like clockwork, as the gypsum in the Sheetrock produced a chemical reaction that soon cleared up the ponds. Once the pond was clear, we'd take coontail plants from some of the clear ponds we fished, once again in a five-gallon bucket of water, and distribute the vegetation into the new pond to provide natural filtering to keep the pond clear. Once the pond was clear, the sun would be able to penetrate the water, and photosynthesis could take place so the aquatic plants could take hold. I guess we were shade-tree wildlife biologists and didn't even know it at the time. I find it amazing we could do all that by just reading outdoor magazines or extension service manuals published by Oklahoma State University. Nowadays all you have to do is google it and then go to YouTube to see how it's done.

Taking it one generation further, in much the same manner that Christopher Camuto discusses in his Trout Unlimited publication, my family is well on its way to keeping the Friedemann fly-fishing tradition alive and well. My son Jim has done a wonderful job of involving his middle daughter, Audrey, in the sport. Audrey already ties her own flies, and I've personally caught some nice rainbows on some patterns she has tied. One of my most treasured moments is that of receiving a Christmas gift from her of six flies: two each of Hare's Ear Nymphs, Woolly Buggers, and Royal Wulffs, all neatly displayed on a piece of rolled-up Styrofoam she constructed. A few months later, I caught a sixteen-inch rainbow on the Woolly Bugger she tied, while fishing Oklahoma's Blue River. Let me tell you, there is nothing more rewarding than catching a fish on a pattern tied by your granddaughter. The trips to the Blue with my son Jim and granddaughter Audrey rank among my fondest memories and have been properly journaled for future generations of Friedemanns to enjoy.

My daughter Kari's oldest son, Nathan, has shown an interest in fly-fishing as well. My wife Cindy and I took Nathan to the Federation of Flyfishers Southern Council's Annual Conclave in Mountain Home, Arkansas—the same event I had taken my son to many years earlier, when he was first developing his skills as a fly-fisher. Grandson Nathan was an instant hit with the expert fly-tiers who were demonstrating their skills to conclave participants at the event, as they typically looked for kids in the audience to give their finished flies to. Of course, there weren't many kids Nathan's age at the event, since it meant taking off from school, but my pitch to my daughter was that the education he received at the conclave would far exceed anything that he could have learned at school that day. He left Mountain Home with a good inventory of flies tied by experts and a passion for fly-fishing. Following the conclave, my good friend and fellow fly-fishing buddy Bob Verboon took us out on the White River in his drift boat, where Nathan was able to test his developing skills on the browns and rainbows in that river. Then, on the way home, we stopped by Flint Creek, near the Arkansas–Oklahoma border, to see whether we could pick up some native smallmouth bass. A picture of Nathan in the middle of a casting motion while wading the Flint that day is proudly displayed in my man cave in

Jones, Oklahoma, along with a picture of Audrey and me wading the Blue minutes after she netted a spotted bass.

I see a little bit of Kari in Nathan and a little bit of Jim in Audrey as both begin their journeys to become accomplished fly-fishers, and it makes me feel good to know that my passion for fly-fishing will live on through them for another generation. It also gives me great comfort to think that someday they may be reading my journals, learning from them, and enjoying my experiences along with me as if I were still there with them.

Granddaughter Audrey with a rainbow trout on the Blue River.

Grandson Nathan honing his fly-casting skills on Flint Creek.

CHAPTER SEVEN
LIVING ON THE WATER

Living on or nearby water has always been a priority for me. On the farm, our pond and nearby creek were always a short bike ride away or within walking distance. Then, when I married and moved "to town," I had the occasion to experience life without water for the first time in my life, and it wasn't very much fun. There is something about water that restores my soul and gets my batteries recharged. Even during the cold Oklahoma winters, which at times can be very severe, just knowing I can put on my winter coat and walk down to the water to get some fresh air is always comforting to me.

My first school administrative position was at the Great Plains Technology Center in Lawton, Oklahoma. My good friend and fishing buddy Bruce Gray had just accepted the position of superintendent at the school and had convinced me to leave my hometown of Stillwater and come work for him. It turned out to be one of the best decisions I ever made from a professional standpoint, and it also afforded me an opportunity to become acquainted with the many lakes and ponds in the Wichita Mountains Wildlife Refuge, which was just a few minutes away from our new home in Cache, Oklahoma. While we didn't live on the water, I was only a few miles away from the refuge and all the wonderful wildlife it contained. One of our favorite Sunday afternoon pleasures was taking a drive on the refuge and seeing bison, elk, or longhorn cattle roaming free. Part of that drive might also include eating at the Old Plantation in Medicine Park or eating a buffalo burger at the Meers Store at the other end of the refuge, or taking a drive up Mt. Scott, where one could see forever. Of course, much of my free time was spent fishing, and there was one spell, according to my logs, when I fished twenty-eight days in the month of March. It was easy to get home from work, load my belly boat into the truck, and get out on the water for a couple of hours of fishing before dark or supper.

One of my favorite places to fish on the refuge was Quanah Parker Lake. After parking my truck in a turnout area near the lake, I took my belly boat and made the short walk to fish. It was a hot summer evening, and the fishing really got good about the time the sun was beginning to set and remained good until dark. I got out of the water, feeling pretty good about all the success I'd had fishing, and then realized that a herd of bison had decided to settle down for the evening between the lake and my parked truck. Now, one of the first things the locals will tell you when you move out here is that the bison are wild and you never want to mess with them, as every year a tourist gets injured while trying to get too close and personal with them. Well, I interpreted "messing with them" as possibly disturbing their slumber by trying walk through the entire herd with my belly boat. After studying the situation for a while, I determined that the only way to safely get to my truck was to circle around them by walking through some tick-infested wilderness and approaching my truck from the rear. It took me over an hour to follow this route, but I got there safely, which was the ultimate goal. However, I had some explaining to do to the wife when I got home as to why I was so late. A cell phone would have been handy back then, but that technology was still a few years away.

After moving back to Stillwater to work for the state career and technology department a second time, followed by one last career move to Oklahoma City to work at Francis Tuttle, the divorce happened. I moved into an apartment for a while, but as soon as I could afford to do so, I purchased a home on a residential lake, and my happiness meter immediately began to register off the scale, as all the stresses of work could seem to be solved just by sitting on my deck in a comfortable chair with a Jack Daniel's and 7UP and gazing at the water and observing the abundant wildlife. My first waterfront home was just off Rockwell Avenue and Hefner Road in northwest Oklahoma City, only a short five-minute drive from my office at the Francis Tuttle Technology Center. It was there, as a middle-aged adult, that I truly began to reflect on the important things in life, and I did most of it while on my dock. "Eagle Lake" is the name the developers gave the lake, although I never saw an eagle on it.

When you live on a lake, you have an opportunity to see wildlife every day, and at times you witness some bizarre behavior that you wouldn't even see on *Animal Planet*. For example, there was one time when I was out early one summer morning in my Hobie Cat and noticed out of the corner of my eye a drake mallard that looked as if he were doing an imitation of an Olympic swimmer training for the two-hundred-meter breaststroke. As I rowed closer, I could see the duck was using only its wings to swim and that it was stopping every twenty feet or so, apparently from fatigue. Now this is where it really started to get weird, because every time he would stop to catch his breath, he would slowly begin to sink. I remember saying to myself, "How could this be? Ducks don't sink!"

It wasn't until I went in for a closer look that things began to start making some sense. As I neared the struggling duck, I could see beneath the water that a very large slider turtle had one of the duck's feet in a death grip and was trying to pull him under. The turtle was so determined to catch this tasty meal that he was willing to be pulled around the lake until the duck ultimately drowned. Talk about possibly biting off more than you can chew! The whole thing was very entertaining, and I spent a few moments just being a spectator to this remarkable animal tug-of-war in which the turtle would nearly pull the duck under. But whenever it looked like the duck was done for, he would somehow regain his energy and resume towing the turtle around the lake. I was amazed that my presence only a few feet away did nothing to take the turtle's mind off his intended prey.

After a while, it became clear that the turtle had the advantage and was gradually wearing the duck down. It was at that point that I made the decision to assume the role of a referee in a heavyweight boxing match and step in before someone got hurt. I gently tapped the turtle's shell with one of my oars, and he reluctantly released his grip. The mallard instantly exploded out of the water like a Polaris missile launched from a submarine and took flight, sounding a stream of quacked profanities that only Donald Duck could understand. He was no doubt very relieved to be free of such a grim ordeal. I'll always wonder what happened to that duck and whether he had any reservations from that point on about sticking his feet in the water. As for the turtle, my hope is that he eventually forgave me for taking sides that beautiful summer morning and spoiling what surely would have been his meal of a lifetime.

Another evening while sitting on my dock, I observed some bass fry jumping up and slamming into my sea wall along the shoreline. This seemed like another odd observance until I took a closer look and saw that a dozen or so channel cats had cornered the fry up against the sea wall and seemed to be taking turns having their way with them for lunch. I had no idea that channel cats were that aggressive or had the kind of intelligence to surround their prey much like a pod of dolphins might do with a school of herring. Once again, I observed this phenomena for a while, but when I realized that these guys were eliminating some prize game fish from the lake, I walked up to the house and retrieved a garden rake from the garage to disturb the water enough to scare the catfish off. I kind of hated involving myself like that with nature, but successful bass spawns are special, and I felt as if my lake needed all the bass it could get. Besides, if they were really that hungry, the channel cats could go next door, where my neighbor regularly fed commercial fish food pellets to all takers from his dock.

Eagle Lake also provided the only opportunity I ever had to observe predictable bluegill feeding behavior during a june bug hatch. In midsummer, my back lawn always seemed to have an unusual number of june bugs, and on those nights, around dusk, the really nice bluegills in the eight to ten-inch range would become active and hit any popper I could throw that looked similar to a june bug. It was very similar to trout responding to a mayfly hatch, only the item on the menu this time was june bugs. Once again, it was one of those experiences that occurred only because I had the good fortune to be sitting on my dock one evening, observing things happening on the lake.

Another thing I saw while living on Eagle Lake that was pretty neat was a snake orgy—or at least that's what it looked like. I went out to my dock to fish one evening after work and noticed that in the middle of a brush pile I had constructed for fish habitat, between the seawall and the dock, there was one huge snake with about a dozen smaller snakes completely clustered around it. I assume that is how they mate, but it was still fascinating to watch and was something that I never would have experienced if I hadn't been living on the water. I don't know what kind of snakes they were, but having seen a cottonmouth before, I knew they weren't poisonous, which made the observation safe and more enjoyable.

Lastly, I remember encountering a huge snapping turtle that evidently had left a nearby pond or lake and was headed to take residence on my lake. Before then, the only time I had ever seen one of these prehistoric creatures was in the water, but this guy was on dry land about twenty yards away from the water. Of course, I had to get a stick and poke at his head to try to measure the power of his bite, and I found it to be enough to assure me that he could take off a finger if he came in range. But what really fascinated me about him was that as I walked around him to study his features more closely, he would rise up on all fours and turn with me. He always kept his front to me, staring at me eyeball to eyeball and hissing the entire time. What a remarkable animal. After my curiosity as to what made him tick was satisfied, I returned to the house and let him enter his new lake without any further interruptions. I saw him a few times after that while fishing and felt as if our little encounter had entitled me to call him a friend. For some reason, I always felt as though he had the same feelings toward me.

After Cindy and I married in 2009, we purchased a home on another residential lake just two miles away from my previous home on Eagle Lake. This lake was called Blue Stem; it was larger and had many more interesting features, such as tree-covered islands, necks, points, and coves. Another plus was not having nearly as much sea-walled shoreline. And instead of a wooden dock like I had on Eagle, our new home had a really cool dock made exclusively of native sandstone. I was excited about spending some time learning a new lake. Cindy is a native of Florida and also a water person, as she grew up sailing the Indian River on the Space Coast, so it didn't take any convincing at all to confine our search for a new house exclusively to waterfront properties. The backyard of our new house had a beautiful canopy of huge trees growing around it, and this, in fact, is where we got married. It was a beautiful outdoor wedding right by the water—perfect for two water people. Our street was called Beaver Creek Road, and it didn't take me very long to figure out how it got its name. One day when I was out in the backyard enjoying the fantastic view we had of the lake, I looked over to my left and saw that our neighbors had a swimming pool. Oddly enough, I had never noticed that before even though we had lived there for a few months. Upon closer inspection, I found out why. In a single evening, a beaver had come and cut down and completely removed three large Leyland cypress trees, revealing our neighbors' backyard, which had previously been beautifully hidden by those same three trees. We then learned that beavers were a frequent problem in the neighborhood, to the extent that the homeowners' association actually had a trapper on retainer that our dues paid for. Of course, we called him immediately, and he soon caught the culprit in a snare. Cindy was so mad that she googled recipes for preparing beaver meat, but she didn't find any. She loved those trees and wanted her revenge and thought eating the enemy would be the ultimate way of getting even. For the next ten years, we lost three more trees to these ornery varmints, but we eventually learned to live with the situation and wound up putting chicken wire around the trees we treasured the most. At least with each missing tree, it enhanced our view of the lake, which was some consolation.

Blue Stem Lake was an excellent lake for producing strange fish that I had never seen in an urban lake. One time while sitting on our rock dock, I saw a gar cruising back and forth, and I immediately ran to the man cave to fetch a fly rod and see if I could get her to strike. One of the rods hanging on the rod rack was prerigged with a Polar Fleece Minnow, and I thought it was as good a pattern to try as any. To my surprise, she charged at it on the first cast and was even on for a short period before she eventually shook the hook. Darn, that was another potential species for my wall of fame. I would speculate that the snout was just too hard for the hook to penetrate thoroughly. I never saw her after that. Gar are native only to Oklahoma's largest lakes and rivers, and there weren't any rivers that fed our lake, so how she got there was quite a puzzle to me. Another anomaly was the presence of warmouth bass, which I caught frequently though they are supposed to be in only the eastern part of the state. Freshwater drum were also part of the lake population—another species that typically were found in rivers and large reservoirs. I found out later that one of our neighbors was a bass tournament fisherman and kept every nonbass species he caught in his livewell and released them into our lake when he returned from one of his tournaments, thus explaining why we had all these fish in our lake that weren't supposed to be there. The diversity of fish added to the charm of living on this lake and to the excitement of never really knowing what I was about to catch.

Following a forty-nine-year career as an educator, I made the decision to retire. Cindy and I sold our home on Blue Stem Lake and moved out to the remote edges of Oklahoma City east of I-35, to a home in the country near Jones, Oklahoma. Water, of course, was a prerequisite to any property we looked at, and we found the perfect match to our needs in a gated community. Our home shares a small lake with four other residences and was created when the developers constructed a dam on Tinker Creek, a tributary to nearby Lake Arcadia. I've already had an opportunity to have some success with both channel catfish and bass in the winter months on my new lake, and I'm really looking forward to learning how to fish it more effectively, as well as nearby Lake Arcadia. I'm excited about the prospects of adding another species to my wall of fame from Arcadia, as the Oklahoma Department of Wildlife Conservation has stocked saugeye, a species I have never caught.

I plan to die living on this lake, but if the situation ever occurs that I need to be in an assisted living center someday, I've already scouted out some places in Oklahoma City that are located on a lake just a short wheelchair ride from the facility.

CHAPTER EIGHT
ALWAYS BE READY

My first job following my graduation from Oklahoma State University in 1970 was as a marketing education teacher/coordinator at Putnam City West High School in Oklahoma City. P. C. West was a new school in a growing part of the city, and this was a premier teaching position. I felt very fortunate to have been selected to begin my career in education at such a beautiful facility just a stone's throw away from the shores of Lake Overholser. What was to follow was a rewarding forty-nine-year career as a teacher and administrator in career and technology education. Part of my teaching responsibilities as a marketing education teacher was the organization of a Distributive Education Clubs of America (DECA) chapter. I was a teacher for only four years, but during that short time, we were able to have the top DECA chapter in the state for two consecutive years and were the runner-up to that recognition another year. That got me noticed by state officials, and after my fourth year of teaching, I was asked to go to work for the Oklahoma Department of Career and Technology Education as the assistant state supervisor for marketing education and the state advisor for the Oklahoma Association of DECA. As luck would have it, the headquarters for the state agency was located in my hometown of Stillwater, so I jumped all over that opportunity.

Living in Stillwater not only gave me an opportunity to

watch my kids grow up in the same hometown where I had been raised but also provided an opportunity to build our family's dream home on my parents' farm and in close proximity to all those wonderful ponds my cousin and I fished when we were boys. After having multiple positions in the department, I eventually rose up through the ranks and became assistant state director for career and technical education. In that position, I was responsible for creating career-tech centers throughout the state of Oklahoma. During that time, we created ten centers at various locations, primarily in rural parts of the state. This meant spending countless hours in local communities with local leaders to coordinate all the steps necessary to put working career-tech schools in their towns or cities.

All my positions at the state agency required a great deal of travel. That often meant spending many evenings in motel rooms with a lot of time on my hands after five o'clock in unfamiliar surroundings. I quickly learned that nearly every Oklahoma town had some good local public access fishing nearby and that if I carried a pack rod in my car with an assortment of some of my favorite flies and lures, I could use that time to catch some fish. Thus, I learned early on in my career about the joys of mixing business with pleasure. So while some folks caught in a similar situation miles away from home might visit a museum, dine at a fancy restaurant, or order room service and watch a movie on TV during those long evenings in strange places, I would get in my car, grab a burger at the local Sonic drive-in, and head for the water.

After nineteen years at the Oklahoma Department of Career and Technology Education, I had the opportunity to become the superintendent and CEO for the Francis Tuttle Technology Center system, with multiple campuses located in Oklahoma City and Edmond. This was the highlight of my professional career, as it was the most envied career and technology position in all of Oklahoma, as well as nearly every other state in the Union. It was great to be at the top of the food chain in a rewarding career where we were changing lives every day by giving people the skills necessary to make a good living and participate in the American dream. While statewide travel in this new position was greatly reduced, I still had the opportunity to travel throughout the country to attend national meetings and conferences, and by that time, I was well aware of how I could make the hassles of job-related travel less stressful and, in the end, make myself more effective for the professional responsibilities I would encounter during the day.

My son Jim, who is a successful management consultant and executive coach, has also adopted the "always be ready" approach in his work, which takes him all over the country, and it has paid off handsomely for him at times. Once, on a trip to Syracuse, New York, he noticed a retention pond between his Hilton Hotel and a manufacturing plant and was glad he had packed his fly rod. He said he felt kind of weird bringing his fly gear down the elevator and approaching someone at the front desk and asking if it would be okay for him to fish the pond that evening. Without hesitation, the clerk said, "Certainly, but I wouldn't eat any of them!" Jim gave it a try, and after having some fun catching several eight to ten-inch largemouths, Big Bertha exploded on his Clouser deep minnow, shocking him beyond belief. She was a healthy four-pound bass who had been waiting for something that she had never seen before to be thrown in her direction. He's also had numerous occasions to travel to Colorado on business, with the hope of possibly filling in some slack time for an opportunity to fish some nearby streams. On one trip to Broomfield, Colorado, he found a local fly shop and was given directions to nearby Boulder Creek. To his delight, he was able to find some willing eight to ten-inch browns in some attractive-looking pocket water right next to a heavily used walking trail. I wonder how many locals have jogged by that creek and never had a thought of ever fishing it. All it took was googling a local fly shop and getting advice on where to go in his rental car.

On one occasion, while serving on the board of directors for the National Council of Local Administrators (NCLA), I had a national conference scheduled at the Maumee Bay State Lodge in Ohio, on the shores of Lake Erie. Cindy and I went two days early, before the conference. We flew into Cleveland, rented a car, and took the scenic drive along the coast to the state lodge. The first day there, we asked the concierge at the lodge about some local fishing, and he directed us to some nearby ponds on the property, where Cindy and I caught a number of largemouth bass in the ten to twelve-inch range. The ponds were beautiful and reminded me of the ones I fished in Oklahoma. I suspect the ponds hadn't been fished much and were deprived of the benefits of a regular harvest, because all the fish we caught were small and nearly identical in size, characteristic of an overpopulation, but it was still fun to catch some "buckeye bass." I remember that I lost a favorite fly—the only one I had for the trip—in an overhanging branch. Because it was right next to the lodge, I asked one of the staff if they would be okay if I waded the pond to try to retrieve it. He indicated to me that he would prefer I not do that because of liability issues, but he asked me where I had lost it. I pointed in the general direction, describing the tree that swallowed my fly, and the next day, he delivered the fly to me. Talk about room service! I never asked how he got it, but I was so impressed with his customer service that I asked who his supervisor was so I could write a letter of appreciation and commendation when I got home. The next day, Cindy and I went to a local outfitter and asked about any public access areas to fish the nearby Maumee River and received detailed information along with a quickly constructed hand-drawn map showing how to get there. He pointed out two options, and we fished both of them. The first spot on his map was known for its walleye fishing, but we were well past the peak season and didn't catch anything, though Cindy and I gave it the old college try. I remember wading chest high in some really cold water on unpredictable terrain and watching Cindy struggle to get to a particular spot; I thought to myself, "Man did I marry well." How many fishermen with my passion for the sport had a partner who would spend (what for her was) a vacation freezing in strange water to get to some good fishing? What a catch she is!

The second suggestion highlighted on the homemade map was a recreational picnic area called Orleans Park just outside Toledo. We drove there and found a much more fisherman-friendly stream with small ripple falls scattered throughout. We didn't need our waders to adequately fish it, and that was nice. The action was slow, but I did manage to catch a nice smallmouth on a pattern I designed, which made that catch extremely gratifying. I have to say that when the conference began the next day, I was in a perfect frame of mind to get the most from the presentations that would be offered by career and technology leaders from across the nation. Fly-fishing has truly become a professional asset to me, much like golf is for many other professionals.

There is another occasion I recall when I took a day of annual leave following a statewide meeting at Oklahoma's Western Hills Resort and Conference Center, where I learned a valuable lesson. My good friend Bob Verboon and I decided to fish below the dam of Fort Gibson Reservoir near Waggoner, Oklahoma. I waded, sometimes waist deep, across the river to the other shore and began fishing after not having any success on the previous side of the river. Then the siren sounded warning that the Corps of Engineers was going to release water. This was my first time fishing below the dam of any lake, and I didn't realize how precarious of a situation that could be. Well, as they began releasing water, I began catching fish for the first time that morning, and I got so caught up in the excitement of catching fish that I lost track of what was happening around me. Bob, on the other side of the water, yelled at me that I had better start back across the river, but by that time it was nearly too late. I was amazed at how different everything looked as tried to get back the same way I had come. I can recall trying to remember what I read in books on how to survive stepping in over my head and floating feet-first down the river for who knows how long, hoping my wading belt was fastened tightly enough to produce a large enough air pocket to keep me afloat. I was literally bouncing off the bottom with each step to get to the other side, and while the water got ever so close to entering my chest waders, I was able to make it back safely. That was a valuable lesson learned. Later, when I was telling that story to another fishing buddy, he informed me that when he is fishing below the dam and the horn sounds, he simply puts a twenty-dollar bill under a rock and continues fishing until the water is up to that rock and then starts back. He said, "You won't forget to keep looking at that rock with twenty dollars on the line." I tried it once, and it truly works.

Finally, an experience that I'll forever cherish is a successful outing I had on the day of my father's funeral. Fishing was the last thing I thought I'd be doing on that day. Following the services at Salem Lutheran Church in Stillwater, I had just taken my mother to my sister Susan's house, which she and my brother-in-law Jess had recently built on the family farm and which was within walking distance of the pond I had fished so many times as a youth. We had gathered there to reminisce, as families do following the passing of a loved one, and it was good to see my two nieces Gretchen and Alexis, who lived in Minnesota, and my nephew Dolph, who resided in Wyoming. I had introduced Dolph to fly-fishing as a boy back here in Oklahoma, and now as a young man living in Casper, he was living in the center of some of the best fly-fishing country in the world and was fully taking advantage of it. It was wonderful to see those early seeds I planted develop into the passion he had for the sport, which rivaled mine.

It was about 8:00 p.m. when Dolph, from out of nowhere, said, "Uncle Tom, I'm going to walk down to Grandpa's pond to see if anything is hitting. I don't get a chance to fish for bass much in Wyoming, and I'm leaving early tomorrow, so this may be my only chance to fish for Oklahoma largemouths for a while." Now, this was in August, and it had been the hottest day of the year, with temperatures still close to one hundred degrees. I knew the water in Dad's pond would feel like bathwater, but how do you turn your favorite nephew down for such an offer? The last time we had been fishing together was at a farm pond when he was a boy and still learning how to fly cast. So I reluctantly said yes, knowing that the odds of us catching something were slim to none and Slim had just left the room, but the conversation between us on the water would more than make up for the nonproductive fishing we were bound to encounter. Here's where always being prepared really came in handy. I always carry a fly rod outfit in my truck with a limited selection of my favorite patterns just in case an opportunity like this ever occurs, so I was ready. I had just changed out of the suit I wore at the service and into a nice knit shirt, my favorite shorts, and deck shoes. That was hardly suitable for fishing a pond that had heavy vegetation and required some wading to get to good water, but I made it work. Against all odds, and in the dog days of summer, we each caught a sixteen-inch-bass, his on a popper and mine on a Clouser Deep Minnow. What's even more remarkable is that my fish shortlined me in about 1½ feet of water, striking aggressively like a spring bass. Now, what kind of self-respecting fish would do that on the hottest day of the year? The only answer I have is that Dad had something to do with all of that and took great pleasure looking down and seeing his son and grandson fishing together again—and in his pond! He wasn't about to let us get skunked on the day we had devoted to honoring his memory.

I have had other countless memories of those times when I used that same pack rod that is always stored in my pickup truck or packed with my luggage to catch fish during a business trip to who knows where. Always being prepared has kept me from ever having any regrets of seeing an attractive-looking fishery at a strange location with enough spare time to fish, but having no gear anywhere around to at least give it a try.

CHAPTER NINE
THE RIVER NEEDS MOWING

Former Oklahoma City mayor Mick Cornett was always fond of saying that his city had the only river in the country that needed to be mowed four times a year. The North Canadian River, which runs through downtown Oklahoma City, was at one time tree-lined with numerous bends. But it had a tendency to flood vast parts of the city during heavy rains, so it was straightened to accommodate heavy water flows. It worked, and the flooding stopped, but what was left was an ugly stretch of dry land that needed occasional mowing because of its inability to hold any appreciable amount of water. In 1993, through the visionary leadership of another Oklahoma City mayor, Ron Norick, a proposition for a one-penny sales tax to fund an initiative called the Metropolitan Area Projects, or MAPS, went before a vote of the people. The proposition passed, and the tax revenues from that initiative launched a renaissance for Oklahoma City that would soon make our city a success story that became the envy of the nation.

The projects that were made possible as a result of MAPS were many and included, among other things, an arena worthy of attracting an NBA team, a river canal similar to what is in San Antonio, a new convention center, and a massive downtown city park. One of the MAPS projects was to create a lock-and-dam system on a seven-mile stretch of the North Canadian

River that would create a series of river lakes, making the stretch navigable. It was a tremendous success, as housing developments and industry soon followed on the shores of once unproductive land. Additionally, biking trails would be developed and a recreational boat district created. What was once an eyesore was now a scenic part of the city and point of pride for its residents. The seven-mile stretch of locks and dams was later renamed the Oklahoma River. What was once a dry riverbed now provided world-class rowing opportunities and even had a man-made white-water rafting section that attracts white-water enthusiasts from all over the world. But what wasn't anticipated was the wonderful fishing that those river lakes would soon provide. I discovered it by accident one day when I was surfing the internet and ran across a message board titled "Oklahoma River Fishing." I thought to myself, "You've got to be kidding me." While the river maintained a healthy water level year-round, it was still in downtown Oklahoma City, and on its best day, the water clarity was marginal and always had the stain of our Oklahoma red clay—not exactly an ideal setting for a serious sport fisherman, let alone a fly fisherman. But these guys on the message board, who evidently worked at a local business that bordered the river, talked about walking down to the shoreline on their lunch breaks and catching fish of all kinds. This I had to see.

It was midsummer, and most of the fishing had slowed down considerably in all the fisheries I typically fished, so I thought, "What the heck, I'll give it a shot." It was a hot and muggy morning, and the sun had yet to rise as I loaded my Hobie Cat onto my truck for the fifteen-minute drive to a loading ramp just off Southwest Fifteenth Street near the Dell Computer call center located on the banks of the river. I thought, "I won't catch anything, but I probably won't have any luck wherever I go, so at least it will be an adventure."

The ramp was right next to the Portland Avenue bridge, which is a major artery of the city. As I rowed my kick boat under the bridge to begin fishing the north shore, I thought to myself, "This is an urban fishery, and I just hope I don't see any dead bodies floating around." It was still dark and actually kind of scary. But that feeling soon went away, as it wasn't too long before I felt a strong tug on my line. Darn, a fish I missed because I wasn't ready for it. I hadn't really planned on getting a hit so soon. I hadn't really planned on getting a hit period. And what was it? In a major river like this one, it could have been anything from a gar to a bluegill. On the very next cast, I hooked into a fourteen-inch largemouth bass who savagely hit my homemade white Road Runner Streamer. To my delight, she even jumped twice. She was a stocky, healthy-looking fish and was decently colored for being a resident in this cloudy, mud-stained environment. I was excited, to say the least, and couldn't wait to make my next cast. I floated down the north shoreline all the way from Portland Avenue, going west toward Meridian Avenue, which is about a mile, catching a variety of fish all along the way.

Once I got to the Meridian Avenue Bridge, I rowed across the river and fished the south shoreline on the way back to where I had launched earlier that morning. It took about three hours to cover that much water, and by that time the temperature was already approaching triple digits, so my timing was just about perfect. Most of the seven-mile stretch of the Oklahoma is lined with riprap, but the last mile between Portland and Meridian was left in its natural condition and contained every type of cover a fisherman could want, including tree laydowns, grassy flats, log jams, and confluences with smaller creek tributaries. I wound up catching six largemouths, three channel cats, one drum, one hybrid striper, and a bluegill. What a nice mixed bag—something that rarely happens in a single outing. I was hooked.

As I was loading up my Hobie Cat, an eighteen-foot bass boat coming from the opposite direction was approaching the ramp. The behemoth rig looked about as out of place on that river as a box of Krispy Kreme doughnuts at a Weight Watchers meeting. I waited for them to load their boat and then walked up and asked them if they'd had any luck. The driver said, "Oh, we always have luck on this river. When it's too windy to fish a large reservoir or we don't have enough time to drive two or three hours to an out-of-town lake, we come here. I've caught bass as large as five pounds on the eastern end of this river." Wow! What a hidden gem right in the heart of the city, and one of the best kept secrets in Oklahoma.

Since that initial visit, I've come back many times, and I have yet to get skunked, although nothing yet has approached the five-pound size. What makes this fishery even more remarkable is its productivity during the dog days of summer, when in most lakes the fishing is slow or nonexistent. The water on the Oklahoma during the spring looks like beef gravy from Grandma's pot roast and doesn't even begin to clear up until late June, so summer seems to be the best time to fish it. One of the fishermen in the bass boat that day went on to tell me that the best fishing was actually in the east end of the seven-mile stretch near Bass Pro Shops, but that was another twenty-minute drive from my house. Part of the appeal of this stretch was the proximity to where I lived at the time, which was on Blue Stem Lake. With my recent move to Jones, Oklahoma, the east end of the river is now actually a little closer than the west end, so I guess that section of the river should probably be put on my bucket list. But it will likely have to wait for a while until I've sufficiently learned the local waters of my new surroundings in Jones.

The Oklahoma River is indeed an urban treasure that is close to home for Oklahoma City anglers. I wonder if the pre-MAPS version of it was what a local fly-tying club had in mind when they named their group the Prairie Fly Fishers.

CHAPTER TEN

ROARING RIVER STATE PARK, CASSVILLE, MISSOURI

I came from a very pragmatic family whose motto was "Use it up, wear it out, make it do, or do without." And what that meant for my sister Susan and me was that if it wasn't necessary, we just didn't do it. Fortunately, my parents always felt like a family vacation was a necessity for all of our hard work on the farm, so we took a short trip somewhere close by every August, just as soon as all the plowing was done. Because Dad would always need to get someone to do the chores while we were absent, he didn't feel comfortable staying away from all his livestock for long periods at a time. We found the perfect spot for a three- to four-day vacation in Roaring River State Park, nestled snugly in the Ozark Mountains in Southeast Missouri. It had everything we needed to make it seem as if we were much farther away than we actually were. It was only a five-hour drive, was out of state, was a complete change of scenery, had much cooler weather, was close to Branson (which at the time was just beginning to develop its music and entertainment industry), and, most important of all for me, had a river full of rainbow trout.

It seemed we would usually go with one of my uncles and aunts, which meant there were cousins to play with, which made it all the more fun. And to make things even better, the motel where we would always stay had a swimming pool, and that was huge! It was during the times we went with Uncle Chuck and Aunt Emma that I really got into fly-fishing. Although I can't remember ever actually catching a fish on a fly rod, just watching my uncle master his rig was absolutely fascinating. He always used an automatic reel, and I can still hear the magical sound of his Martin reel sucking up the slack line the minute he had a fish on. I watched him much like a young little leaguer might watch Mickey Mantle take practice swings in the batting cage. He was a sight to behold indeed.

Uncle Chuck and me fishing side by side on Roaring
River. I'm watching his every move.

As a new family, Jo and I continued the Roaring River tradition while our children, Jim and Kari, were growing up, and we would also go with my cousins and their families to replicate my childhood experience for our kids. But then, when the children got older, we found other places to go, such as the ocean, ski trips to the Rockies, Oklahoma State University bowl games, and even Hawaii.

I didn't reconnect to Roaring River until Cindy and I had married and she asked me to go with her to her class reunion, where she received her bachelor's degree from William Woods University in Fulton, Missouri. When I looked at the map, I saw that it was pretty close to Cassville, and I convinced her to drive by Roaring River State Park on the way back home. As we began the long descent to the river, my heart started racing just like it had years ago, and I was amazed at how little the entire park had changed. It was seemingly frozen in time. The spring that emerges from the top of a steep limestone cliff directly above a big cave, was still there, constantly dripping water from another age into the river, as was the hatchery, and so was the original park store where I would buy my Woolly Worms that I would connect to inline spinners. Even the night-before ritual of buying a daily trout tag was still identical to the way it was done back in the '50s. And except for the increase in price, I don't think they had even changed the tags themselves. The river looked exactly the way I had always remembered it, which was a comforting thought in this day of rapid and sometimes chaotic change.

At that point, I knew I had to come back again soon. That next summer, Cindy and I took a little fishing vacation and stayed at the lodge and convention center that had been recently added. And just as I had as a ten-year-old, I nervously stood by the river with my fly rod and waited for the horn to sound, signaling it was time to make that first cast.

A few years later, I took Jim and A. B. with me to revisit the river because I knew they had similar pleasant childhood memories of growing up fishing there. They, too, couldn't believe how little it had changed. In fact, we lodged in the same Rock Village Court Cabins that I had stayed in fifty years prior, and except for some updating, it hadn't changed much either. Oh, the memories it brought back of seeing Uncle Chuck's 1954 Packard and my dad's 1953 Ford parked outside the cabin, side by side, in standby mode, waiting to take us to the river at six o'clock the next morning. The smell and sound of the water and the chill in the August morning air as we waited for that same horn to sound all came back and brought great joy to my heart.

To keep those feelings of joy, I have since organized an annual fly-fishing trip that occurs in the spring during the first week in May. But it didn't start out as a Roaring River deal and had to go through a bit of evolution first. Let me explain.

Back in 2006, my good friend and fellow church member Gordon Knox and I thought a good way to encourage Christian fellowship would be to organize a fly-fishing trip. We would later call it the Flyfishers of Men Retreat. Our first three trips were to Oklahoma's Lower Illinois River, near Gore, Oklahoma, in the eastern part of the state. Since many of the men didn't know how to cast a fly rod, I conducted a series of classes on the back lawn of the church and provided all the gear for those who didn't have a fly rod. On our first trip, we had twenty-two Lutheran men attend, and I spent the entire time basically providing guide service to those who needed it. It was a huge success, as nearly all the men caught fish. We stayed in adjoining cabins at MarVal's Resort and Fish Camp and had some great times every evening consuming adult beverages (remember: these are Lutherans) and swapping stories of fish caught and fish lost. What was amazing about that first trip was that although it was primarily a trout fishery, we caught eight different species of fish during the three days of fishing, including a four-pound largemouth bass one of our guys, Terry Mock, landed using an olive Woolly Bugger. I didn't get to fish much, because I spent most of my time untangling lines, tying on flies, putting on new tippets, netting fish, and giving fishing advice when needed. But it was a ton of fun watching all the guys I went to church with every Sunday share my love for the sport and have some success on the water.

We continued to go to MarVal's and the Illinois for two more years. Our last trip there was not nearly as much fun, because of a heavy water release every day we were there. The heavy water flow basically took wading out of the picture, and not a single trout was caught over the entire three days of fishing. I could tell the guys were pretty frustrated, and there was even some talk of possibly canceling the following year's trip because of the uncertainly of water releases by the Corps of Engineers. I didn't want the event to go away, so I proposed a new location: the Lower Mountain Fork River in southeast Oklahoma, near Broken Bow, Oklahoma. A very good friend of mine, Dian Jordan was manager of Pine Meadow Cabins, a consortium of luxury two- and three-story cabin owners who would rent them out to help defray the cost of ownership. Dian really wanted our business and made us a sweetheart deal by providing the cabins to us at a very competitive price in an effort to entice our guys to give it a try. Compared to what we had at MarVals, these were like staying at Ritz-Carltons, with Jacuzzis, pool tables, gas grills, and big-screen TVs, which were great for the evenings since the Oklahoma City Thunder were always in the NBA playoffs and the guys all enjoyed watching the games each evening after an exhaustive day of fishing. That first year, we beat our attendance record, and the guys had a great time, with nearly everybody catching fish. By this time, most of them were requiring less personal assistance, which freed me up to do more fishing. And that was a good thing. Guide service is hard work, and I was doing it for free.

We continued going to the Mountain Fork for another seven years until a major flood took out most of our favorite areas to fish. That's when I made the decision to move the Flyfishers of Men Retreat to Roaring River, but first I would need to make sure they had enough cabins to accommodate a group our size. That was the same year Cindy and I took our little vacation to Roaring River, and one of the things I wanted to do, besides fish, was scout out their cabins. I did, and they turned out to be a perfect fit for us. Our first year of having the retreat at Roaring River was 2015, and I don't think the group will ever want to go anywhere else, because (1) we don't have to wade, which for some of our older guys is becoming as issue (2); it generally takes less skill to catch fish; and (3) there is a golf course nearby for some of our guys who are golfers first and fly-fishers second, in case they want to spend a day on the links. While the lodging is a little more expensive than at the other two places, I think we're at Roaring River to stay, even though much of the Lower Mountain Fork has been restored and the fishing is close to being back to normal. It's also comforting to know that a place I was first introduced to by my parents, uncles, and aunts is still playing an important role in my life. It's just good for my soul to return to this special place each spring!

Organizing annual fishing trips like this one and the fall trip we do to Red River in New Mexico can really be a fun and rewarding experience—especially if you have the right dynamics in your group, which we seem to have achieved with both outings. But I think organizing two of them is my personal max. Any more than that and someone's going to have to start paying me.

CHAPTER ELEVEN
RED RIVER, NEW MEXICO

Years ago, on a family skiing vacation to Taos, New Mexico, I had the opportunity to share a chair lift with a Taos native and struck up a conversation. After learning that he had an annual ski pass and had taken the afternoon off from work to get in a few hours of skiing before heading home, I commented how lucky he was to live so close to a ski resort and lamented, "I wished Oklahoma had a ski resort."

To that he replied, "You do; it's called Red River." He said the locals never ski there because the Texans and Okies have taken it over. At the time, I had never been to Red River, but cousin A. B. had many times—not to ski, but to fish—and was always telling me how beautiful the country was and how great the fishing was, even during the summer months. A few years later, I got a call from Orb Hulsey, superintendent of the Caddo-Kiowa Technology Center in Ft. Cobb, Oklahoma, who said he was trying to get a few guys together who would be willing to go in on purchasing a cabin that was for sale on the banks of the Red River in New Mexico. Split with five other buyers, it was affordable, and I jumped all over it. It turned out to be one of the best purchases I've ever made. All the owners were career-tech school administrators, so we knew each other well and had a high level of trust, which is always essential to every partnership. But I was the only one who was a passionate fisherman. The others wanted the property for either skiing, enjoying the mountains, or just having a place to go during sweltering Oklahoma heat in the summertime. Each year, we would draw for the dates we wanted, and being the only fisherman in the group, my prime picks in the fall, when the trout were most active, were always open, so it worked out beautifully.

I bought into the partnership with only photographs to look at, but the first time I had an opportunity to use it, I couldn't believe how perfect it was. It had three bedrooms and two bathrooms, with plenty of room to host a second family or a group of four to five anglers. And one could literally fish from the back porch; that's how close it was to the river. As a matter of fact, it was so close to the water that when I contacted my local agent in Oklahoma to insure the property, he refused because of its close proximity to the river. Thinking I may have made a major mistake in purchasing property that was at risk of rising water, I then went to a local agent in nearby Questa, who didn't hesitate to insure the property, saying he knew that area and we would never have to worry about that part of the river going outside its banks, which obviously made me feel much better. I've had the property for twenty-six years now, and even during the heavy snowmelts, we've never had a problem with flooding.

One of our first trips from the Red River cabin partnership was a family vacation with bass fishing buddy Bruce Gray and his wife, Patricia. We did all the touristy Red River things, but Bruce and I couldn't resist the convenience of having a river just outside the cabin. Now, as I mentioned earlier, Bruce was a bass purist and fished only with conventional gear, and by this time I had converted exclusively to the long rod, which I don't think Bruce ever quite understood. When we would fish in Canada, he would always tease me about fishing for small perch, and he gave me a nickname "Swish-Swish" in reference to the noise the rod made going back and forth several times in the wind while making several false casts before I loaded it for the actual presentation.

The Red is quite narrow by our cabin, and in most cases, one could spit a watermelon seed from one bank to the other with some luck, or wade it with a good pair of galoshes, so Bruce just couldn't see much opportunity to catch the fish of the size he was accustomed to catching from his bass boat. But there was this one big, deep hole about fifty yards upriver from the cabin that I knew could hold some really big trout. So one afternoon when everybody else was sleeping in the cabin, I went to the hole and, to my delight, caught what at the time was the biggest rainbow of my life—a twenty-one-inch fish caught on a Pistol Pete. And while I was already into catch-and-release at that point, I just had to walk it to the cabin and wake everybody up to take a gander at it. We took some pictures of with me holding it, and by the time we had done all that, she had been out of the water far too long to survive a release back to the river, so we wrapped her up in paper and put her in the freezer. That puppy was getting mounted! Bruce was in disbelief. He had never seen a trout that big and reluctantly admitted, "Now that's a fish, Tommy Bill," using another nickname he had for me.

Two days later, during a constant light drizzle, we all took an afternoon nap again, but this time it was Bruce who went to that same hole, trying to see if lightning would strike twice in the same place. Bruce was probably the best bass fisherman I had ever been around, and he always prided himself in one-upping anybody he fished with. After someone caught a fish that surely seemed would be the trip fish, he became energized to catch one bigger. He loved having the last at bat. And what was remarkable about Bruce was that I can never remember a time when we were fishing that he didn't follow through. Without exception, he would always have landed the biggest bass at the end of the day. But that was lake fishing for bass, and now we were stream fishing for trout, and he was, after all, on my turf now. When I woke up and saw him fishing in that same hole, I almost felt sorry for him, knowing there was no way that hole would produce another lunker trout on the same trip. But guess what? It did! It wasn't thirty minutes later that Bruce knocked on the door of the cabin and shouted "Tommy Bill, come look at what I got." Sure enough, just like the days when we may have been fishing for smallmouths in Canada or for largemouths in Oklahoma, he one-upped me again. There he was, holding a twenty-four-inch rainbow caught in that same exact hole on his ultralight spinning rig using a chrome Super Duper. The look on his face reminded me of the look on Brad Pitt's face when he played the youngest son in the movie *A River Runs Through It* holding a huge rainbow he had just caught after a terrific battle, showing it off to his father and older brother. I thought to myself, "This guy truly is the best fisherman I've ever seen, and it doesn't make any difference what species you're after; he's going to beat you."

Of course, his trout also was beyond surviving that amount of time out of the water, so we once again wrapped it in paper and put it in the freezer. Later we decided to have them both mounted together on a piece of driftwood, and to this day they are hanging above the fireplace in the cabin as a memorial to a very dear friend who a few years later would be diagnosed with cancer and taken away from us much too young. Every time I go back to the cabin and look at those two fish with both our names on brass plates under them, I cannot express in words the joy the memories of all our fishing trips together bring to my heart.

Bruce Gray with his big rainbow trout caught just outside our cabin in Red River, New Mexico. As always, he outfished me on that trip.

Another summer, three of the double cousins all went to Red River in our SUVs, and we all had a marvelous time together: Cousin A. B.; his wife, Lanette; and his family; Cousin Patty; her husband, Jim; and her family; and I, with my first wife Jo; and our family. A highlight of that trip was an excursion we all made to Goose Lake, an alpine lake whose access road was about one hundred yards or so southeast of our cabin. So our three families crammed into Cousin Patty's Ford Explorer and my Jeep Cherokee and made the seven-mile trip straight up and over some of the scariest terrain I would ever care to encounter again.

It took us just over two hours to reach the end of the trail, but waiting for us when we got there was beautiful Goose Lake. The guys all had good success catching rainbows in the ten to fourteen-inch range, and we made the trip back down in good shape without any issues. But it wasn't until we got back to the cabin that I realized I had left my gear bag back at the lake. When we discovered this, the others all had blank looks on their faces afraid to ask me what I was going to do, because they all knew I had a small fortune invested in the fly-fishing gear that was in that bag, but nobody was about to volunteer to go back with me to try to retrieve it, mainly because this was a vacation and was supposed to be fun—and that second trip was not going to be fun.

So, testing fate, I began the trip back with just Jo this time, because nobody else wanted to make that treacherous trip again, especially with someone at the wheel who was obviously very upset with himself and the situation he was in. But I wasn't about to start from scratch all over again to replace all that gear. I knew I was taking a bit of a chance and that the bag might not still be there, but because of the remoteness of the lake and difficulty of getting there, I was pretty sure it would still be where I left it—and fortunately it was. That memory is etched in stone in the back of my brain. From that point on, my OCD went out of control, and now I can't go anywhere without checking around the area we were fishing at least a dozen times before I'm comfortable leaving. I'm sure to this day that I'm the only person on the face of the earth that has made two trips to Goose Lake in the same day.

A few years later, Jo filed for divorce, and I began a year of searching for the next chapter of what my life would look like. My son Jim, still a bachelor at that point, had spent a week at the cabin the year before and had a great time going back up to Goose Lake and further exploring the area that the local chamber of commerce calls the Enchanted Circle (the area surrounded by Red River, Taos, and Angel Fire). Jim encouraged me to take some time off work and make a solo trip to reflect on life and get my mind right. That fall I did just that, and the results of that trip, probably more than anything else, set me back on a positive course in preparing for life after the breakup of a thirty-one-year marriage.

Besides doing a lot of meditation and reflecting, I did some exploring and scouting around for good fishing spots. After having some success catching trout on both the Red and Cimarron Rivers, I thought I'd try for something different and visited Starr Angler Fly Shop in downtown Red River and asked the owner where I might be able to catch some northern pike. She said about the only place one could probably find pike around there was in the Rio Grande, and the best way to access that river was to take the road that goes to the John Dunn Bridge. She drew out some directions, and I was off to the Rio Grande the next day. Finding this place takes an act of faith, because for the longest time you feel as though you're going into someone's driveway; at some points you can literally touch adobe huts from the window of your vehicle.

The Rio Grande during the fall is a marvelous fishery with consistent water flow and deep holes throughout the river for as far as you have the energy to walk. If you decide to fish streamers, which I did, you pretty much need a sinking-head line to get down deep. My fly line of choice was a Teeny T-200 matched with a 6 weight rod. When I got there on the first day, there was someone just leaving, and I asked him if he'd had any luck. He replied positively and told me that if I just threw a streamer of any kind, as long as it was black and yellow, I'd have some success.

The only thing I had in black and yellow was an ancient marabou jig that I had purchased as a boy back at Roaring River in the 1950s. So I tied it on for this big hole right under the bridge and almost immediately got into something really big. It felt more like a catfish than a trout because it just stayed deep and kind of sulked, as if I'd snagged a log. But I could tell by feeling a constant head shake that it was a fish of considerable size. I was sure I'd hooked a pike, because I couldn't imagine a trout behaving quite like that. After a lengthy fight, I realized that it was a big brown, a variety of fish that had eluded me early in my fly-fishing journey. I was excited beyond measure when I finally netted her and got a picture taken of her next to my fly rod on the grass. She measured nineteen inches and was by far the biggest brown I had ever caught up to that time. I went back the next day and continued to catch numerous browns and a few rainbows, although they weren't near the size of that first fish. I never did catch any pike, but I certainly wasn't going to complain.

What was to happen the following day was something straight out of a *Law & Order* episode. I was the only one on the water that weekday morning and was wading waist deep several pools down from where I had caught the big brown earlier in the week. I noticed that a small compact car was racing down the road and across the John Dunn Bridge and parked opposite from where I was wading. I didn't pay much attention to it until a pickup truck came by and stopped next to it. That's when things got interesting. There were two females and two males who began yelling at each other, and I could tell folks were very upset. Then I heard gunshots and saw that one guy was chasing the other male around the pickup truck, and the girls began screaming. A second and third shot was fired, and then the pickup sped off down the road.

Some thoughts that immediately went through my head were (1) "Did anybody get shot?" (2) "Did anybody die?" and (3) "Did the shooter look around for any witnesses and maybe see me standing waist deep right across the river and decide, 'I need to take this fly-fisherman out so he can't testify in court about what he saw?'" I didn't know what to do. I didn't have a phone, and I wasn't the most mobile, being in waders and in the water. It seemed like no time before there was an ambulance there along with two patrol cars. They marked the area off with yellow crime scene tape, so I eased up a little at that point and continued to fish, but not with very good focus on what I was doing. About an hour later, one of the patrol cars drove across the bridge and parked next to my SUV, and a highway patrolman came up to me and asked if I had seen anything. I described what I had seen but wasn't sure whether I could ID the shooter because of the distance between me and where the shooting took place. He told me that the two women were willing to talk and would make good witnesses, and that the authorities probably would not need me in court to testify as to what I saw. But he took my name, phone number, and the address of the cabin and asked me to stay in New Mexico for a few days just in case. Fortunately, I was going to be at the cabin for two more days anyway, so that wouldn't be a problem, but I thought I'd better be prepared to stay longer if necessary or perhaps make a return trip to New Mexico sooner than I had planned in case I was to appear in court. The trooper also said that it looked like the victim was going to be okay and that it was probably a drug deal gone bad.

Time passed, and I never heard anything back, but it certainly was an experience that I will never forget, and every time I go back to that area to fish, I think of how a place so peaceful and beautiful could instantly turn into a crime scene one might expect to encounter in downtown Chicago! At any rate, the trip overall was a wonderful experience and served as a catalyst for a return to Red River with some fishing buddies every fall for an annual fishing trip.

Yellow tape marks the crime scene overlooking the Rio Grande.
An unwelcomed intrusion from the outside world into paradise.

That solo trip in the fall of 1998 laid the groundwork for what
was to become an annual fishing trip with four other fishermen
that included my son Jim, Cousin A. B., and two very dear friends,
Bob Verboon and Chuck Nithman. All of us are dedicated fly-
fishers, and I cannot recall us having a single disagreement in
two and half decades of making this annual trip. It's such a joy
when you don't have to walk on eggshells because you're afraid of
upsetting someone, and that's certainly the case with this group.

I met Bob while I was working at the State Career and
Technology Department in Stillwater and he's the one who kept
encouraging me to get into fly-fishing even before I saw "the
movie." Bob is the best nymph fisherman I have ever fished
with and has the patience of Job. He is always trying to figure
out new complicated and difficult-to-cast double nymph rigs
with insanely small flies and tippets. What's worse is that we're
oftentimes forced to switch to these complex rigs because of

his success in using them. Bob is also a gifted taxidermist and mounted a thirty-nine-inch northern pike I caught in Canada on a Whitlock's Deep Sheep and a twenty-two-inch rainbow I caught using a fly I designed that I call a Ginger Bugger during one of our annual trips to Red River. Both fish are proudly hanging in my man cave in Jones.

Chuck attends the same church I do, St. Paul's Lutheran in Oklahoma City. He is a gifted rod maker and is responsible for making my favorite rig of all time: a ten-foot three-weight rod he made using a TFO blank, perfect for dead drifting dry flies and nymphs. He also made portable fly-tying stations for both Jim and me. Chuck is a very studious fly angler and is always giving the rest of us great insights as to why the fish are behaving the way they are. And if there ever was a Nicest Man of the Year Award, Chuck would have my vote, as he is abundantly generous with both his time and resources and is constantly performing acts of kindness for the rest of us.

I've already talked a lot about A. B., but one thing I haven't mentioned is his passion for Tenkara fishing, or Eastern-style fly-fishing, as he calls it. He can catch more fish using that method than you could ever imagine. He must have over twenty different types of Tenkara rods and carries about a half dozen of them, all rigged with different flies for the various situations he finds himself in. The Tenkara rod industry needs to recruit him as their poster child, as there isn't a more passionate Tenkara guy anywhere.

I've previously talked a lot about Jim and am not sure what I could add except that he has the sweetest casting motion of anyone I've ever fished with. I mean it's right out of a Mel Krieger flycasting video. He's far surpassed me in that skill, and I can only watch in awe every time we're out fishing. Jim, at A. B.'s encouragement, has also become a big fan of Tenkara and uses it frequently to enhance his enjoyment out on the water.

Each one of these four guys is a superior fly-tier. They are far superior to me and not afraid to take on the patterns that are really difficult to tie. The patterns they tie or design look as if they came straight out of an Orvis catalog. Once again, I stand in awe of the skills they have in being complete fly anglers and people I am honored to be able to fish with on a frequent basis.

The trip to Red River is always set for the last week in September and is usually perfectly timed with the aspens being at their peak color. As with any annual trip, we've made modifications to our routine while experimenting with different places to fish, to the point that now we typically concentrate on five fisheries: Red River, Cimarron River, Rio Grande, Rio Costilla, and Rio Hondo. All of these places are within a thirty to sixty-minute drive from the cabin, and all have produced handsomely throughout the years. We've also tried Springer Lake and Eagle Nest Lake in pursuit of pike but with no success, although we've had our lines bitten off by pike and caught some beautiful yellow perch. My son Jim even caught a nineteen-inch rainbow on Eagle Nest one year using a bright pink #1/0 pike fly attached to a stainless wire leader with a snap. I thought rainbows were supposed to hit small patterns and were tippet shy. Go figure! I remember that rainbow as being badly beaten up, with bite marks and exposed flesh everywhere and looking more dead than alive, but she gave Jim a terrific fight and jumped several times before he landed her. We figured she had been in a life-and-death struggle with a big pike and barely survived. Her chasing something that big was a quick way of getting a huge chunk of protein to help her on the way back to health.

As with any series of annual trips over the course of that much time, we were bound to have some that we'd just as soon not repeat, and three specific trips quickly come to mind. One year, Chuck wanted to hire a guide to explore parts of the Cimarron that we might be missing. We had never felt the need for hiring a guide in the past, but it did seem like a good way to learn more about the Cimarron. In typical Chuck fashion, he insisted that it be his treat and refused any reimbursement. That particular year, Bob and Jim were unable to go, so it was just the three of us: A. B., Chuck, and me. Our trips usually involve three days of fishing, and Chuck had the guide booked for the second day. We decided to fish the Rio Grande the first day. The fishing in the water close to the bridge had been really slow that morning, and following our shore lunch, I thought I'd try an area downriver about a half mile, at a honey hole that had been productive for me during past trips.

We finished our lunch from the comfort of our collapsible chairs, and I began the long, difficult hike downriver. A. B. and Chuck decided to fish the same water, thinking they could eventually figure it out—which, of course, is one of the most enjoyable parts of fishing. When I arrived at one of my all-time favorite spots on the Rio Grande, I immediately began catching some nice browns, and I stayed in that general vicinity for the remainder of the day. As the shadows from the deep canyon ridges began to cover the water, I started back toward where our vehicles were parked. I had completed the most difficult part of the hike and had my destination in sight when I stepped into a hole and fell down with my foot still in the hole, resulting in what I thought at the time was a high ankle sprain. Ouch! It really hurt, but with the help of a makeshift crutch I found nearby that a beaver had conveniently made, I managed to limp back the rest of the way, thinking it was just a bad sprain. I thought a little bit of ice and a good wrapping would be all it would take to make it feel better the next day.

That evening, the swelling continued, and so did the pain. I kept it on ice until we went to bed that evening. I was fortunate in that Chuck was a pharmacist and happened to have some bandage material with him, and he professionally wrapped my foot and ankle. While it felt pretty good following Chuck's magic, I wasn't looking forward to being on it all day. I kept the crutch I found on the Rio Grande and used it to get from one spot to another the entire day. Being in tight-fitting wader boots and standing in cold water all day helped to keep the pain and swelling in check, but I was a burden to the others and had a difficult time keeping up with them as we moved from one spot to another.

Our guide's name was Ed Adams. Ed was a great guy and took a special interest in me because of my physical situation. And it was that disability that may have resulted in me catching the trip fish of the day and my personal best on the Cimarron, a fourteen-inch brown. Ed always made sure he put me on the best holes, where I wouldn't have to move much to catch fish. He would then leave to check on A. B. and Chuck. One nice run he put me on had a deep cut into the bank with brush hanging over it. His instructions were to somehow put my size 20 Adams fly just above that cut and let it run under those branches, with the bold prediction, "If you can do that, you'll have yourself a take." Well, as luck would have it, I miraculously made the perfect money cast and watched the Adams float almost out of sight under the branches, and wham! There she was, a nice fourteen-incher, just as Ed had predicted. It almost made me think the fish and guide were in cahoots. We were both pretty proud. By the end of the day, the ankle was worse, and we again iced it up for the evening.

On the last day, we made the sixty-minute drive to the Rio Costilla, and none of us caught any fish the entire day, but we didn't try all that long. The river is a tailwater, and the engineers decided to quit releasing water that week, which pretty much ended any hopes of our having a good day there. The Costilla is gin-clear anyway, and with no runs available to fish, it just wasn't going to be a good day; so we quit early, which was fine by me because the pain from my ankle seemed to be getting worse. The next day, we headed home. Without ice or the ability to raise my leg while driving, the pain became almost unbearable, to the point that I asked Chuck to take the wheel while I elevated the leg for the rest of the trip. I went to work that following Monday but by Wednesday realized I might have more than just a bad sprain, as I hardly recognized my foot from all the swelling. I went to my doctor the next day, and X-rays revealed that it wasn't a sprain at all but a torque break of my fibula. I wound up wearing an orthopedic air walker boot and using a knee scooter for the next four months. While I would never want to go through that experience again, it was something I can boast a little bit about. What a manly man I was to be able to fish for two days on a broken leg. I still have that beaver-made crutch, which I affectionately named Wilson after the volleyball Tom Hanks befriended in the movie *Cast Away*. It hangs today in the man cave as a reminder of how someone's passion for something can overcome pain and adversity.

Another annual trip that wound up in misfortune was one we had where my Honda Ridgeline broke down just outside of Slapout, Oklahoma, which is exactly in the middle of nowhere. Bob left from Red River to go straight to Wyoming for a hunting trip, and A. B. stayed in New Mexico, where he was going to meet his wife later for an extended stay in the Rockies, so it was just Chuck, Jim, and me. As a group, we probably had one of our best trips ever in terms of catching fish, and we were all headed home happy and content from three days of fishing the waters that we all love so much.

Jim was driving at the time when the truck suddenly lost power and came to a slow stop on the side of the road. Thank goodness for cell phones, because there wasn't a house within sight and it was beginning to get dark. After calling my insurance company and having them get a tow from the nearest provider, which was in Woodward, Oklahoma, we just sat there wondering what our next step would be. All of our wives were either out of town or unavailable to come get us, so we decided that after we got a tow into Woodward, we would just spend the evening there and try to rent a car back to Oklahoma. There was no Honda dealer in Woodward; in fact, all the car repair shops were closed the next day because it was Saturday, so we knew there wouldn't be any waiting until the truck got fixed to go home. Jim and I both had a full day of work scheduled for Monday, so we were in a terrible fix.

Finally, Chuck was able to get ahold of his daughter, who graciously picked us up at the car repair shop where the tow truck left my Honda, and she took us for the final two-and-a-half-hour leg of the trip back to Oklahoma City. It was probably close to 2:00 a.m. before we got to bed that evening. And moving everything from my truck into Chuck's daughter's SUV in a dark parking lot was nerve racking as well. Chuck volunteered to drive me back to Woodward to pick up my truck about two weeks later. We never did find out what went wrong. The mechanic sprayed starting fluid into the fuel injection system to get it running again but couldn't get the truck to duplicate what it did near Slapout. Since I was the superintendent of a career-tech school, I had easy access to a highly-trained automobile technician faculty and asked them what they thought went wrong. They even got a regional Honda executive involved, but none of them could figure it out either. The best logical answer seemed to be bad gas from a fill-up we did in Clayton, New Mexico, even though we drove for four hours before the engine died. Another theory was a faulty fuel pump, but that checked out okay as well. The mechanic in Woodward told me to burn premium fuel with no ethanol in it for a while and see if it did it again. It never did, and over the next two years, we drove it to Red River two more times, with everything going perfect. But I never trusted it fully the entire time on both trips, and eventually I traded it for my dream vehicle, a Jeep Gladiator pickup.

A third trip, which also ended badly but wasn't a part of the annual all-guys fall fly-fishing trip, was one that Cindy and I took where we never even made it to Red River. We left immediately after work, planning to stay that evening in the historic Brown Hotel in downtown Springer, New Mexico. That evening when we went to bed, I got up around midnight with a terrible pain in my side that kept getting progressively worse. I took a hot bath, which helped some but provided only temporary relief. After a sleepless night, we left at the crack of dawn for home, as it was pretty evident I needed to go to the emergency room in either Taos or Boise City, which had the closest hospitals to Springer. We opted for Boise City in the Oklahoma panhandle, since it was on the way home.

It was just outside of Clayton that I correctly self-diagnosed what was wrong. I had a kidney stone. I'd had one back when I was twenty years old, so I pretty much knew what the symptoms were, and the situation wasn't good. The only way I was going to get any relief was to get a shot of a high-powered painkiller, and that was hours away. By this time, Cindy was driving, and I was asking her to put the pedal to the metal. She was probably going close to ninety miles per hour, almost hoping we'd get stopped by a highway patrolman so he could legally blaze a path for us to Boise City, sirens blaring. To try to take my mind off the pain, I was listening to satellite radio, and it had just been announced that John McCain had selected Sarah Palin as his running mate, and the pundits on the cable news networks were all over it, so at least there was something interesting to listen to.

When we got to Boise City, it was interesting, to say the least. Boise City is a rural Oklahoma town of about twelve hundred people with one doctor. It has a town square and is probably the closest thing Oklahoma has to *Mayberry, R.F.D.* I expected to see Andy and Barney walking out of the sheriff's office at any moment. The hospital had a single floor, and there were about three people ahead of me in the waiting area. When I finally had the opportunity to see the doctor, I was startled to see that he was probably in his mideighties (about the same age as my dad) and quite a character. As a way to become better acquainted with me, since I obviously was not a local, he remarked, "I've been cooped up in here all day. What's going on in the outside world?" I told him that McCain had just announced who his running mate would be—Sarah Palin, the governor from Alaska. His eyes brightened up, and he said, "Oh, that's wonderful; I've been keeping up with her career, and that's exactly what McCain needs—a young, energetic female to balance the ticket. I am absolutely delighted."

He then proceeded to strike up some other nonmedical conversation, to which I replied, "Hey, Doc, I'm kinda in a lot of pain here; could we take care of that first?"

"Oh, of course; I'm sorry, son, he responded. What type of pain are you feeling?" I told him where the pain was, described how it felt, and said that I was pretty sure it was a kidney stone, because I'd had one about forty years ago and it had felt the exact same. After doing some probing around my middle core, he said, "Yep, that's probably what it is all right. Kidney stones—they ought to reserve those bastards just for Democrats!"

After doing some lab work, he gave me a shot to immediately address the pain and prescribed some oxycodone, and we were on our way back to Oklahoma City. I was very soon in much less pain. Thank you, God, for Boise City, for salt-of-the-earth eighty-year-olds, and for painkillers. I passed the stone a few days later.

Those three unfortunate incidents of course pale in comparison to the joy of owning a cabin in the Rockies next to a river, but even paradise has its ill fortunes sometimes. Now that I'm retired, my hope is to get out there more often and experience the all the benefits that mountain living has to offer. I'm told there are other things you can do out there besides fish.

CHAPTER TWELVE
GINGER BUGGERS AND OTHER THINGS WITH HOOKS

I think we'd all agree that fly-fishing is more than just learning how to use a fly rod and being able to cast it. There's the understanding of the various lines, tippets, and flies; reading water; understanding habitat; entomology, etc. But for me, fly tying is the icing on the cake. While most spin fishermen I know would be in dire straits if they couldn't go to their local Bass Pro Shops or Cabela's to stock up on the latest lures designed and manufactured by someone else, fly anglers seem to think an integral part of their breed of angling is making the doggone thing yourself. To us, a landed fish means so much more if it was attracted to something we made ourselves. And it's even better if it was a fly of our own original design or a pattern we improved or modified.

My fly-tying skills are not very good, but fortunately for the vast majority of situations, the flies I tie don't need to be fly-shop quality. In fact, some of my most productive patterns are often those flies I'm a little bit embarrassed to show my buddies when that inevitable question comes up: "What are you catching 'em on?" Many times the response that follows is "You're kidding me … on that?" So thank you, fish, for not being as picky as some fly-fishing guides and authors would have us believe.

The first fly I learned to tie was a Woolly Bugger, I and immediately began having success with it on bluegills, which quickly built up my confidence to continue on to other patterns. The second pattern I learned to tie was a Clouser Deep Minnow, and I experienced good luck with it as well. I then began experimenting with color combinations and hook sizes that weren't found in the local fly shops. The next stage of my fly-fishing evolution was to go on to exotic materials that I could find around the house, in the backyard, or on the side of the road. One of the prettiest Clousers I've ever tied was made from a dead skunk that got hit by a car in front of our house. Before carrying it off, I held my nose and clipped all the white hair I could from it. Over the next few days, I tried all the remedies suggested by a Google search to eliminate the smell and found that none of them worked very well, but that didn't deter me from my obsession to use my free fly-tying materials somewhere. After my final attempt to wash away the smell, I examined it further and noticed that the hair had a texture similar to that of bucktail, the same material used to tie Clouser Deep Minnows. I tied a few Clousers with it, combining the white hair with some bright orange bucktail, and those flies turned out great and have become some of my most effective for bass.

On another occasion, when I was getting ready for a trip to Manitoba to fly fish for northern pike, I tied some giant patterns using hair I extracted from Buck, the family golden retriever. Man, Buck's tail looked great in the water and some good-sized pike in the Winnipeg River thought so too. The only problem with me doing that was having to deal with some personal guilt I had from making him self-conscious about the way he looked for a month or so until the hair on the end of his tail grew back. I don't think it was any accident that all the female dogs from the neighboring farms pretty much stayed away during that same time period, which just added to my feelings of guilt.

And if you know any hunters, you'll find that they are usually willing to donate feathers toward your hobby from a recent pheasant or duck hunting trip. Of course, sometimes you have to listen to them brag about their trip, but it's well worth tolerating to get the free fly-tying materials. Another ready source of materials was my dad's cattle and chickens, which were always readily available just a short drive from my house. A brief stroll around the farmyard is like a visit to your local fly shop. You can make a dandy-looking Woolly Bugger from the feathers of a Rhode Island Red rooster.

Designing your own flies is fun as well. The more you fish and observe what's going on, the more you come up with ideas of patterns that might work. The first and most successful attempt at fly designing came from a trip my son Jim and I took to the Lower Illinois River near Gore, Oklahoma. We didn't have a lot of success that day but noticed three guys who did. I mean, they were catching trout one right after another. None of them could have been older than thirty. I noticed they started heading toward their vehicle to go home, probably from arm and muscle fatigue as a result of catching all those fish. Here was my opportunity to learn about their magic formula for success. I learned a long time ago that a sure-fire way of becoming a better fisherman is to just ask those who are having a lot more success than I am what they are using. If there is one thing I have learned about fly-fishers throughout the years, it is that they are always eager to share their success. So I asked. The oldest of the three didn't hesitate to show me a simple jig he was using with a strike indicator, and he graciously gave me his. It looked really simple to tie and was nothing more than some ginger dubbing wrapped around the hook of the jig, with a ginger grizzly marabou tail.

I guess it was the ginger color that got my attention. While I tied some just like it the next day, I got to thinking that I had never seen my favorite streamer at the time, a Woolly Bugger, tied in that particular color or tied on a jig hook. I wondered how that would work. I began doing a little experimenting and came up with my own modification of what I call a Ginger Bugger (because that's the only color I tie it in). Here's how it's different from a typical bead head Woolly Bugger: First, I start with either a $\frac{1}{124}$, $\frac{1}{80}$, or $\frac{1}{64}$ ounce jig in either a chrome or gold color. And rather than wrapping the body in chenille, I use wool yarn, which seems to trap air underwater and give the body a translucent look. I tie in a ginger marabou tail, but I leave it much longer than those used on traditional buggers. In fact, the tail of my ginger bugger is slightly more than twice the length of the body of the fly, measuring from the jig head to the bend of the hook. I then palmer ginger hackle around the body, and presto! What this results in is a woolly bugger variation that I think looks a great deal like a sculpin darting from rock to rock.

At the writing of this book, I have yet to see anything like my Ginger Bugger in fly shops or mail-order catalogs. Over the years, I've given them away to numerous fly fishermen and even a Montana guide who seemed intrigued by the design and asked if he could have one. For many years, it has been my go-to pattern when nothing else seems to work. The trip fish I've caught on this pattern include my personal best rainbow trout, a personal best walleye, my second-biggest brown trout, and several really nice largemouth, smallmouth, and spotted bass. It's a great pattern for both warm-water and cold-water species. Every fly-fisher has in his mind what the one fly would be if there were a law that said an angler could take only one pattern to the water, and my choice would be my trusty Ginger Bugger.

Another pattern that I designed—and one that's been successful, especially for bass—is something I call a Road Runner

Streamer. I call it that because it looks very similar to the Road Runner baits designed for spinning and baitcasting gear that are manufactured by the Blakemore company in Wetumpka, Alabama.

I tie two variations of this streamer: a shallow version and a deep version. For the shallow model, I use a #2 hook most of the time but have gone up to sizes as large as 2/0. The first step is to attach a split ring to one end of a swivel and then insert the point of the hook through the other end and position the swivel next to the eye. Then glue it to the hook near the eye using JB Weld. I know what you're thinking: "JB Weld? Isn't there something more Orvis-like you can use than that?" But JB Weld works just fine for me. The only issue I have with using it is the need to wait six hours for it to cure. Because of that, I usually cement a half dozen hooks at a time and then let them dry overnight before I begin the next step. Once the cement has cured, I then attach a size 2 to size 3.5 willow leaf blade to the split ring. The rest is easy. Just tie on some bucktail at the head of the streamer just like you're tying a Clouser Deep Minnow, except you don't have the barbells to deal with. For added fish appeal, I will sometimes mix in some flashabou or silicone rubber legs. I don't use anything but willow leaf blades for this pattern, because they tend to spin better with less chance of hitting the body of the fly while the blade is attempting to rotate. Once the JB Weld hardens, it creates a nice little plastic-looking head at the base of the hook eye that is suitable for painting a color that matches the bucktail. I like to think of this pattern as a fly-fisher's version of a spinnerbait. My favorite colors for this pattern are chartreuse, green, yellow, and orange, or any combination of those, which seem to imitate a perch or sunfish. It is particularly effective for smallmouth bass but works well for all warm-water species.

The second variation involves a $\frac{1}{32}$ ounce jig that already has the swivel and spinner attached, which saves you a couple of steps. You can find these in the crappie section of most Bass Pro Shops. The problem with these jigs is that they come with a miniscule size 00 Colorado spinner blade, which I think is next to worthless in creating the underwater disturbance and vibration that makes this pattern so effective. To remedy this, I replace the blade with (you guessed it) a willow leaf blade about twice the size of the original Colorado blade. When I began using this deeper version of the Road Runner Streamer, I tied on a small amount of flashabou about the same length of the jig itself with good success. Later, I increased its effectiveness by adding a soft plastic split-tail trailer that bass anglers sometimes attach to the ends of their spinnerbaits. With this addition, it had great action in the water and was a much better producer than the sparse short flashabou I had been using. One day I was fishing with A. B. on Blue Stem Lake, and he took note that I was just drilling them with my split-tail version of the Road Runner Streamer. The next time we fished together, I noticed that he came up with a modification of this fly by tying twice as much flashabou as my original models had and also doubling the length so that it more closely imitated my split-tail model. I copied his variation, and today that's the only way I tie this pattern. It even looks better in the water than the split-tail version and is a much more consistent producer for both of us. The biggest problem with using a jig that was originally designed for crappie fishermen is that by the time you tie on three inches of flashabou, you wind up with a pretty big four-inch bass streamer with a very small and thin size 8 hook; I've had the hooks straightened out several times by some very large bass. It would be nice if I could go to a larger jig, but then the increased weight of the streamer would be too heavy to cast on a fly rod. It's all I can do now to cast the $\frac{1}{32}$ ounce jig and its oversize blade with my 9-weight fly rod.

One of my favorite patterns for both cold-water and warm-water species is a Pistol Pete, which is made by Hi-Country Flies in Trinidad, Colorado. It is basically a bead head Wooly Bugger with a propeller blade attached to the front. Along with the Ginger Bugger, this guy is one of my go-to patterns when nothing else seems to work, especially in cloudy water. If you can tie a Woolly Bugger, you can tie one of these. Although you can find them at fly shops as large as size 2, I tie even bigger versions that are specifically designed with bass in mind. The bigger versions I tie are on hooks as large as #2/0, with an oversized propeller blade. These larger models have proven to be deadly for both bass and channel catfish. Heck, I even caught a flathead on one in Lake Hefner. Another alteration I often make to my bass-size Pistol Petes is to tie on a soft plastic curl tail in place of the traditional marabou tail. The swimming action of the curl tail combined with the turbulence made by the oversize front propeller is a sight to behold and makes it a completely different fly—one you'll never find in a fly shop or catalog. I call my modification a Curl Tail Pistol Pete.

Finally, a pattern that I originally tied for crappie has turned out to be a killer for bass and catfish when fished behind a strike indicator set at five feet in still water. This pattern is one of the simplest patterns you'll ever tie. Once again, I go to the crappie section at the local Bass Pro Shops and purchase a card of unpainted $\frac{1}{64}$ ounce jigs. I then tie on about 1¾" of chrome flashabou with black thread, and that's it. Twitching it every few seconds behind a strike indicator gives it an unbelievable action. Using a strike indicator—or "interest monitor," as I prefer to call them—allows the pattern to stay in the water for a longer period of time per cast, which also seems to add to its productivity. Channel cats just love them early in the spring, and I've caught some really nice largemouths on them as well. And yes, they'll catch a crappie or two now and again. I call this pattern a Silver Bullet Jig because when it hits the water, it looks as if it came straight from the barrel of the Lone Ranger's six-shooter.

I've designed numerous other flies and have made alterations to other existing patterns that have not been successful, but those failures have only served as a way to make my four superstars (Ginger Bugger, Road Runner Streamer, Curl Tail Pistol Pete, and Silver Bullet Jig) even more special. Coming up with an idea that results in a fly you know nobody else has in his or her fly vest gives one a special confidence when out on the water. And having success with them while everyone else is in envy mode and struggling just to get a hit is about as good as it gets. You know they're eventually going to have to ask, "What are you catching 'em on?" which gives you the opportunity to experience one of the most cherished moments in all of fly-fishing: the opportunity to show off a fly that you designed or modified yourself—one that you know they wish they had. Of course, another cherished moment is offering to give them one of yours so you can watch them share in the fun.

CHAPTER THIRTEEN
NEVER TAKE A NET

My cousin and treasured fishing buddy, A. B., was unloading his SUV as we began the short walk to the pond we were getting ready to fish. A. B. is a passionate advocate for Tenkara fly-fishing, which means he typically uses a much smaller tippet than with a conventional fly-fishing rig, making the net a highly valued piece of equipment in helping to prevent break-offs. Realizing this, I noticed his net was still in the back of his Subaru Outback as he began to close the tailgate. Thinking that I was helping him out, I said, "Aren't you going to take your net?"

He responded, "I never catch any fish when I bring my net."

I eventually persuaded him to take it, knowing that the pond we were getting ready to fish had steep banks and it would very difficult to land a fish by hand, especially with a twelve-foot rod connected to a twelve-foot line, which is how most Tenkara systems are rigged. So he brought it and got skunked for the day! Of course, it happens to all of us.

Superstitions are present in all sports. The Great Bambino, Babe Ruth, always felt the need to step on second base every time he came in from right field following the third out of every inning of every ball game all season long. New England Patriots quarterback Tom Brady wears the same shoulder pads that were issued to him his freshman year at Michigan. He plays with teammates who aren't as old as his shoulder pads. And Michael

Jordan wore the same shorts under his Chicago Bulls uniform that he wore when North Carolina won the NCAA Championship. Others eat certain foods before games or lay out their uniforms in a certain way in the locker room as part of a pregame ritual, all designed to ensure success on the field.

Fishermen are no different. My Uncle Chuck Nida, whom I've referred to numerous times in this book, would always take a brand-new hard-bodied fishing lure he had just purchased at the store and drop it in the dirt and step on it with his shoe, grinding all the new finish off of it before he fished it. He said bass don't like factory smell on their prey. I also heard about a local angler who would never release a fish into the water regardless of how big or how small it was, even if he intended not to keep any for eating. He would either keep them in a fish basket or put them on a stringer and return them to the water when he left for home. His theory was that fish have developed a way to communicate with other fish about their out-of-water experience and that all the luscious-looking prey they'd noticed in the area lately were fake. And as a result of that intelligence briefing, they would put off feeding until all the fishermen left the premises. That's some pretty heady credit for creatures with a brain the size of a pea.

Before cell phones came into play, I would never take a camera with me, knowing that the fishing gods would get upset if I were to become so presumptuous as to think I was going to catch something that day worth taking a picture of. Better to have caught and released a fish that you wish you could have proven to your buddies than to have never caught one at all because she may have been a little camera shy and somehow knew you had one in your fishing vest. I've always wondered how those same gods allowed at-the-ready picture-taking technology to enter into the world of smartphones in the first place. Now nobody has a reason not to have proof of a catch.

According to Merriam-Webster, superstition is "a notion

maintained despite evidence to the contrary." You'd probably have had a hard time convincing A. B. that day that getting skunked wasn't all the evidence needed to prove that having a net close by prevented him from having the kind of day out on the water he had hoped for. And while he didn't say a thing about it, I felt a little bit guilty.

And just like Michael Jordan's shorts or Tom Brady's shoulder pads, fishermen are notorious for having a favorite piece of their uniform. Three-time B.A.S.S. Angler of the Year, Bill Dance would never think of fishing a tournament without his signature University of Tennessee Volunteers baseball cap. The most famous example would have to be the lure-decorated soft-brimmed fishing hat often worn by McLean Stevenson in his portrayal of Lt. Colonel Henry Blake in the hit TV comedy *M*A*S*H*. His hat could have filled a small tackle box.

I have a favorite vest that I finally had to retire just last year. It was made by the Richard Wheatley folks, who have been making fishing gear in England since 1860. I had that vest for over thirty years, and it always contained everything I needed to be successful on the water. Just like a golfer's caddy, it was always there to help me with the most challenging situations. Finally, after the last zipper failed to zip and holes began to appear in the bottoms of the pockets, I had to give it up and go to one of those new age fancy-type vest packs with a built-in lumbar support, built-in life vest, and, at last count, about two thousand pockets, most of which are still hidden at the time of this writing. I still haven't found most of the pockets or the equipment I haphazardly put in them. It looks more like something you'd use to jump from an airplane than something you'd use to wade your favorite trout stream. No telling how many fish I didn't catch because I spent far too much time looking for stuff in one of those darned pockets—time that could have been better spent keeping my line wet. I'm finally beginning to get used to the new vest, but it's taken far more effort than I had anticipated.

And then there is my favorite pair of chest waders made under that famous American brand Red Ball. They were my first quality waders and, like my Wheatley vest, a piece of fishing apparel that I kept far too long. With my Red Balls, I could confidently walk through a briar patch to get to a fishery, which I actually had to do sometimes, and I always felt confident that I would arrive at my destination with waders that would keep me dry throughout the day. But like everything else on this precious Earth, they eventually wore out too. I can't tell you how many times I had successfully patched them with Shoe Goo, but I must have used up three tubes repairing them. They looked pretty gross toward the end with all the scabby-looking patches on them. Oh, the stares I got from other fishermen. I could hear their whispers as they walked by in their brand-spankin'-new, fresh-out-of-the-box Simms G4 Pro Model Gore-Tex Waders. I thought to myself, "Sure you look good, but can you fish worth a lick?" Nothing I've ever owned has lasted nearly as long, and while I really love the new breathable fabrics waders are made with today, I sure do miss my Red Balls.

While fishermen are an odd lot in that they all have their unique ways of approaching the sport with a mixture of skill and superstition, it's not just fishermen who are superstitious. Manufacturers of fishing equipment also are guilty of relying on the supernatural to market their products. The James Heddon and Sons company, out of Dowagiac, Michigan, named one of their most respectable bass lures the "Lucky 13" in an effort to capture some mystic appeal for vulnerable fishermen seeking some supernatural assistance. Thank you, Mr. Heddon, for adding Friday the thirteenth to our calendar as a good day to fish.

I'm sure by now you've probably determined that the focus of this chapter is on the role superstition plays in our beloved sport of fishing. And because you're engaged in reading this book,

I'm also assuming that you're considerably more intelligent than the average angler and likewise noted that it's also the thirteenth chapter. I was warned that books with thirteen chapters won't ever get published. So read into that whatever you want. Good luck, and good fishing!

BIBLIOGRAPHY

Bignami, Louis, Robert Jones, Kenneth L. Kieser, William R. Rooney, Joel Vance. *Wit & Wisdom of Fishing.* (Lincolnwood, IL: Publications International Ltd., 2001).

Buchanan, Mark. *The Rest of God.* (Nashville: Thomas Nelson).

Camuto, Christopher. "Stream Of Consciousness." *Trout* (Summer 2007), 14–15.

———. "Uncertain Weather; Uneasy Seasons: Angling the Anthropocene." *Trout* (Winter 2015), 22.

Davenport, John H. *Get Into Fly Fishing - For Under $100.* (Denver: John Davenport, 2014).

DePree, Max. *Leadership Is An Art.* (New York: Dell, 1989).

Hallock, Blake. *Early Northwest Fly-Fishing: A Fly-Angler's Lifetime Journey Through Oregon, Washington and the World.* (Portland, OR: Frank Amato Publications, 2006).

Houston, Jimmy. *Catch of the Day.* (Nashville: J. Countryman, 2005).

Lucas, Jason. *Lucas on Bass Fishing.* (New York: Dodd, Mead & Company, 1962).

Maclean, Norman. *A River Runs Through It and Other Stories.* (Chicago: The University of Chicago Press, 2001).

Mares, Bill. *Fishing with the Presidents.* (Mechanicsburg, PA: Stackpole Books, 1999).

CPSIA information can be obtained
at www.ICGtesting.com
Printed in the USA
LVHW040810101120
671143LV00005B/491

9 781480 894211